A favourite son of   ⌐wn
Liverpool, Gerry Pott(, playwright,
director, actor, and the   ⌐yer of the infamous
gingham diva Chloe Po(previous publications as Chloe
included *Universal Rentboy* [Bad Press, 2000], *Adult Entertainment*
[Route, 2002] and *Li'l Book o' Manchester* [Mucusart, 2007]. A
former writer-in-residence at Manchester's Greenroom and
Contact theatres, he has a reputation for putting his Scouse
voice on the line, a soaring sing-song accent, and is strong on
poetry and strong on the causes of poetry. *The Men Pomes* is his
third collection of autobiographical, domestic-fantastic theatre-
verse for Flapjack Press.

By the same author

Planet Young

Planet Middle Age

THE MEN POMES

GERRY POTTER

f p

Flapjack Press
www.flapjackpress.co.uk

First published in 2011 by Flapjack Press
Chiffon Way, Trinity Riverside, Gtr Manchester M3 6AB
www.flapjackpress.co.uk

All rights reserved
Copyright © Gerry Potter, 2011

Facebook: Gerry Potter-Poet & Gerry Potter Poet Fan Page
YouTube: Gerry Potter Poet

ISBN-13: 978-0-9570141-0-7

Printed & bound in Great Britain by Direct-POD
Saxon Fields, Old Harborough Road, Brixworth, Northampton NN6 9BX
www.direct-pod.com

This book is sold subject to the condition that is shall not by way of trade or
otherwise be lent, re-sold, hired out or otherwise circulated in any form,
binding or cover other than that in which it is published and without a similar
condition including this condition being imposed on the subsequent purchaser.

Dedicated to Gordon Stark [1964-2011].
Enormous, complicated, extraordinary and fit.

Contents

Foreword by Steve Lyons	9
Introduction	11
Spotty	19
Listen	22
The Killer Pumpkin	14
sometimes the sky	27
Little John	31
The Boogie Man	33
There, That Bloke Under The Tree	35
And Then The Man Said	38
Love Those Frankenstein Guys	41
The Ballad Of Jimmy Butler	43
Comrade Brother	46
Bashed	49
Somewhen	54
A Statue To See-Anne	56
A Little Bag Of Sad	58
Death, Me And A Taxi	60
Jimmy Bling	62
The Shmuck	65
Community Of One	68
Men In The Ink	70
Lonely Seeks Moonbeam	72
Tiny Bangs	75
The Quiet Place	77
How Do You Respect Fuck All?	79
Betting	81
In A Liverpool Moment	84
Folly Butler And Her Bad Man Blues	87
Folly Butler And The Blossom Of Fireworks	90

The Man Crone	92
Gone Fission [for Ken Campbell, 1941-2008]	94
A Middle-Aged Muddling	96
And When I'm Old	97
Gordon [1964-2011]	98
The Telling Man	101
Oh Father	102
Jesus The Babe	103
Elvis, Me And Big-Bang Momma	105
Slap	107
The Magician	108
Cake	111
Of Men	114
Outroduction: Bangs His Chest And Roars War At The Universe	117

Foreword

When I was asked if I'd write the introduction for Gerry Potter's new book, *The Men Pomes*, my first thought was, "Why does a rampant puff from the wrong end o' the East Lancs Road want a miserable po-faced straight laced Manc like me to write it? Surely they'll be queuin' up in the Village 'n' the Northern Quarter to pen some superlatives for champion of the underdog?" Then I realised it's 'cause I'm cheap. In fact, I'll do it for fuck all.

When I first started this poetry lark in the latter days of the last century there were two certainties: at any given poetry night at least three poets would have a version of "The Revolution Will Not Be Televised", 'n' at least half o' those attendin' would ask me if I'd seen Chloe Poems yet? They'd tell me I ought to see Chloe Poems 'cause he's brilliant, 'cause he's the best thing since sliced bread. You know the sort o' stuff. I was determined not to like him. In fact, no matter how good he was I'd hate him. I'd hate him as much as I hated them middle-class soulless versions o' "The Revolution Will Not Be Televised".

The irony of it. When I did finally get round to checkin' him out he was everythin' he'd been cracked up to be, even better, but I was the only person in the audience who thought so. He was drunk, I was drunker (that might of had somethin' to do with it), but the very same people who'd been biggin' him up to me were lowerin' themselves in their seats 'n' squirmin'.

Well, the next day I phoned a few mates 'n' told what I'd seen 'n' heard. Some pissed-up homo with attitude dressed in a gingham frock 'n' he was fucken different from owt else 'n' they gotta see him. Which they did. I don't think they were too impressed at the sight of the anti-tranny transvestite till he opened 'n' had 'em in stitches. Me mate Catt had a mouth full of Guinness when he heard the line "I want to be rimmed by Jesus".

Well, he just burst out laughin', sprayin' the Guinness all over those in close proximity, bubbles o' booze comin' out o' his nose 'n' nearly chokin'. Another friend was so impressed he bought Chloe's book there 'n' then without realisin' what the title was, till I said, "I'm not walkin' round town with you carryin' a book called *Universal Rentboy*. Later, he left it on the table in a curry-house 'n' was too embarrassed to go back in 'n' ask for it.

Sadly, the gingham diva hung up her frocks and put away her wigs a couple o' years ago. Not entirely desertin' us though, she now leaves all the talkin' to her alter ego, Gerry Potter. And very capable he is, too. *The Men Pomes* is his third book of verse for Flapjack Press, 'n' after you've read it no doubt you're gonna want to *buy* them 'n' put an end to the myth that poetry lovers are notoriously tight-fisted. The first two volumes are *Planet Middle Age* 'n' *Planet Young*, 'n' well worth choppin' down trees in the rain forest for.

Keep the faith,
Steve Lyons
Wythenshawe, July 2011

Introduction

God and Satan, they follow me round.

Where I come from men don't say poems, they say "pomes". Women say poems, but I think men feel the word a tad effeminate so they do their best to butch it up. Hence *The Men Pomes*. Pomes could beat poems in a fight.

Blokes, eh... Warrabout 'em?

I suppose this has to start where all things start with me. Although profoundly atheist I can't help meandering through the foggy cloisters of my Catholicism. Men begin there. Men benign there. Men fight there. The first bloke you love's called Jesus and he's perfect, then everyone afterwards is a let down. The men in these pomes stink of religion; not just the religion of bygone churches, but the faith of men. A tricky and haphazard belief liable to have you questioning at every turn.

I was born into a broken fireplace with a band of brothers. The final embers of the church were burning, but had not yet gone out. I remember men in black and white and built from red brick. They were big and loud and knew who they were and what they wanted. They looked great and swaggered, the charcoal of the streets was definitely theirs. When I was born there were hungry men but even hungrier factories. The chug-plod of the sixties was in full bloom and the blossoming smog proved it. Men had shoulders they could carry you on and fists to hit you with. God and Satan in equal measure. Men gave you crisps outside pubs and bottles of Dandelion and Burdock. Men lifted you up to the sun.

The men I'm mostly writing about are working class men. I am a working class man. Well, I'm more a working class effeminate homosexual man, so therefore considered too posh or effete to be a real bloke. I remember once borrowing the girl next door's doll. I hurriedly disrobed it and made an exotic cavegirl outfit for her with my mother's chamois leather duster. She looked great. She could beat Tarzan any day. I was pleased with my creation, so pleased I showed her to one of my brothers. Well, he flipped. I'd never seen him so crazy. He took a butter-knife and stabbed the doll repeatedly till all was left was ruptured plastic, a tattered chamois and hysterical hair. He screamed queer at me and stormed out. That was bad enough, but what was worse was returning the mutilated remains of Sindy to the girl next door. She cried a lot and her ma wasn't too pleased. That same brother would shield me from a storm and step in front of a bullet. That same brother would fart in my face. God and Satan.

I hated being called posh more than I hated being called queer.

When I was seven and eight, and within a very few months of each other, three of my brothers had falling accidents. Two of them fatal. The news of these deaths was cataclysmic to the community around us. It was a maelstrom of grief and we were the eye of the storm. When I was seven, I was to learn very quickly young men die, and they did. The fall-out of those deaths impacts on me still, and, even now I'm much older than those brothers who died, they still tower over me. They are still magnificent and they are men. Much more men than any men I know now. I couldn't write this introduction without you knowing the reality and the myths of these memories. About the lack of longevity in men. A lot of young men died in my area. I don't remember young women dying in the same way. I witnessed the full-on unconditional grief of men. Big men and big boys do cry. These biblical visions of men uncontrollably weeping are etched into my soul. From a very early age I knew men could feel. I saw men hold and support each other through the most crumbling of times. I saw men care deeply and openly.

I've not seen it so much since.

There are a lot of pomes about the sadnesses of men in this book. The griefs and the depressions. Each one different but the same.

Not having a father was to impact greatly. My brothers all had a dad but not me, he ran out before I was born. One of the emptiest moments of my life was carrying my dad's coffin with my brothers. They were grieving. I was lost. Not having a dad didn't do too much for my self-esteem. I have abandonment issues pouring from my arse, but now I adore that man.

I know the drunken dancing of men, the tripping bravado of naked brothers. The chaos theory of partying like tomorrow you might die. I know the robust desire to fulfil a good time. I know why young men let go. I know why they party.

These pomes are a reflection of men. They deal a lot with the simplicity of good and evil. I see good and evil clearer in men than I do women. I was hurt by men. Trounced by their physicality, and, although I love men, I can't forget those moments. I am attracted to the men who hurt me. And when I say good and evil I'm being biblically ironic.

I'm drawn to the struggle of men and the inconsistency of self which pervades them. Times haven't stopped a-changing and emasculation hasn't reached its climax. There's a lot more misguided muscle thugging around now than I ever remember. I see the lost generations of Thatcher, Major, Blair, Brown and Cameron as angrier and far less focused. I think men used to be cleverer than they are now, certainly politically. In these less religious years I see God and Satan more.

The pomes in this book in many ways are simple morality tales. They deal with the magnificent imaginings of men. I think they have potential. They are about the war of men and we can never understand men if we don't talk of war. Although there isn't a war pome in here it is definitely a motif. Huge swathes of men wiped out irreligiously for peace. Doesn't bare thinking about. It's why I couldn't write a war pome. Thinking about the scale of that suffering makes me hate humanity. Men have had a raw deal. I think the race memory of war is why so many young men dance with death.

And I have to mention football. My God, the horror of football. It meant nothing to me but fear. It bored me as a concept and playing it at school was simply an act of brutal humiliation. I was that cliché who was always picked last. Sometimes not picked at all and that was a joy. Once, I had to play five-a-side football in the school gym. I was, as usual, running around aimlessly and camply, never really knowing what I was doing. Somehow the ball landed at my feet. It startled. I kicked the damn thing just to get it away from me. Well, it left my foot and magically landed in the net of the opposing team. The whistle blew and I had miraculously scored the winning goal. Now, whenever anyone scored the winner there would be a surge of approval then a rush to hold the scorer above their heads. Well, there was the surge and cheer but when they realised it was *me* that scored it they all dissipated limply away. They didn't want to hold up the queer. I'd got used to the bullying of school but this really hurt. I did a proper boy's thing, a real proper boy's thing, and still I was shunned. I recognise, however, the great camaraderie of the sport and its effect on mine and the lives of my class. I wanted to write a football pome but I couldn't. Elusive as a war pome, but again it is a motif.

These pieces are not just about working class men, they hopefully stretch further than that. It's just I know working class men better than any other sort of men and if I'm honest they interest me more. I like the lack of intellectual capitalism.

I've been wringing on about my issues with men for a very long time. I haven't finished journeying around them yet. Most of the men I've met have been amazing people, but some of them...

Imagine, if you will, God and Satan fighting it out on the last battlefield. Perfectly matched and counterpointing. Each move and punch a chess masterpiece. Each prayer and roar an opera. They are fighting their last fight. This is only the beginning of *The Men Pomes.*

Gerry Potter

THE MEN POMES

Spotty

Some men are young.
If I could, I wonder what I would tell my young self. I wonder what my young
self would tell me.

Spot.
Look.
Face.
Soft face.
It does a look in the mirror,
It does a look at life.
A squeeze.
Mishmash.
Soft lad!
Cock-eyed and skewiff.
An airplane glade of cloud fuzz.
In there, a place where I'm sat burning toast
Because the conversation's so good,
That blazing fire witnessing legends.
Been spitting stories since flint first hit stone.

SCLICK-SCLICK!

A blade of histories made smoke,
A shaving of smoke,
A dissolve in a film noir flick.
Spot!
Beer froth.
A rip of thought peels away.

I want to know what's right
And shape the future like I can the past.

The past was the future wasn't it?
It's a spot.
Froth.
A clout of ideals smacking away
Trying to tumble accidentally from my chin.

My back aches.
Spot.
Throb.
I twist my body, makes it easier to do, what,
Sit and watch the telly?
Froth.

I want all my opinions table-sat and riveting.
I know there's magic in cauldrons of tea and slurping words.

I hate my imagination and its distances,
There is no community in thin air,
No biscuits.

World seems enormous small.
Have you seen it grow into a man?

Don't want to write torn or ripped or ache
Because someone will call it cliché.

Is it because the world grows into a man it doesn't understand?

Don't want to write understand or hope or pray
Because someone will call it cliché.

Is it because boys grow to men they use the word cliché?

Is it because I will be a man?
Spot the cliché.
Is it all there is?
Spot!

Wish this was a war poem,
Maybe then I could say defenceless.

Spot.
A mote of dust.
Universally nothing more.
Broth.

Spot.
Spot.
Spot.
Spot.

Join the spots and we have a galaxy.
I'm cold in this
Gurning
Froth
And my spots are the smiles making pop art.
If I hang me on my wall
Maybe I'll have something to be proud of,
To smile at.
A universe of acne,
Bed-sit alchemy
Of an all at once,
Of a maybe this time.
A mirror of clocks,
A history of horrors and anarchy.
A time-piece of spots.

Listen

Some men are children.

Give me a raw and angry child,
A bawling boy,
And I'll show you the truth.
He won't be dipped in the honey-dew of melancholy,
The woo-woo of Boo-Boo,
That special space where the fireside
Warmed the cockles of your heart.
He'll be screaming and stomping and so very very right.
And if you try to comfort him
Or tell him things ain't that bad,
To step on the sunny side of the street,
To turn that frown upside down,
Then I will kill you.
You deserve to die.
Let him scream and hear those screams,
Listen to the gothic of his pain.
It's for a reason,
It's for you to hear,
To open your ears and heart.
It's the world bleating out its fear.

You make the men.
You make the men.
Listen!

Don't buy him a gift.
A pair of space-age trainers,
A Tommy-Gun,

Grand Theft Auto.
Please don't make killing an option
Because he'll kill you.
You'll deserve to die.

Don't slap him away,
Slip him a Mickey.
He's not an ailing wasp,
He's not being tricky.
He's human.
So be more human,
Adult human,
And listen.

The Killer Pumpkin

Some men are creepy Halloween.
Twinkies are a famous cup-cake advertised in American comics of my youth.

Out the mist,
Tumbling, a stagger that would impress Karloff,
The Killer Pumpkin dressed in zombie and tradition,
Universals and Americans from the grubby back pages
Of *Weird Tales.*
He's dressed in ink, lightning and fingerprints.
Tangible ink.
Ink that lives under your bed,
Ink you can smell,
Tacky as a sock of spunk,
Strobe lit and *FLASH!*
Comics are not yet computerized,
Still immune to progress,
Are terrified of Communism
And smell of the fifties.

A Bag of Laughs
Cackles.
Fake Blood
Drips.
Charles Atlas and his Dynamic Tension
Muscles in.
Instant Monkeys
Swim
And X-Ray spex
See the skeleton of your hand.
The Killer Pumpkin,
A compelling Santa for kids too bullied to love being kids.

The Killer Pumpkin hovers over the girl,
Blood dribbling from carved lips,
Finger-sticks claw one inch below her breasts,
Withering breath caressing her cheek.
Screams in big white capitals
That spiral from her mouth to the sky
And fly off the page.
Finger-sticks clutch her throat.
It's only ever nearly rape
But it's always blue murder, revenge and rage.

The Killer Pumpkin's unaware he's a drawing,
An animate for the relish of post pubescence.
He's just a soulless plunderer
Waiting for another hapless victim
Or a Twinkies endorsement.
Mmmmmmm, Twinkies!
The Killer Pumpkin's magazine is a little shop of horrors
And a Twinkies delicatessen.
The Killer Pumpkin will one day be king of death,
Nearly rape,
Cup-cakes
And morbid obesity in adolescence.

The Killer Pumpkin kicks at the mist in the cemetery
Of Fox Twentieth Century,
Makes the shapes of Lugosi and Chaney,
Dracula and the Wolf-Man,
Blows them into the full moon.
You've seen their faces,
Carvings from the unhallowed breeze
Of dark arts and imagination.
The Killer Pumpkin will encourage kids to devour television.

The Killer Pumpkin retreats to his lair,
He's killed enough dames to avenge his brutal murder.
Resides in the tomb of Erasmus DeKnight,
A forgotten poet with too much Byron and fervour
Whose name has been eroded from his headstone
By lashing rains and indifference.
They grieve and wail moans and groans.
The Killer Pumpkin kisses Erasmus's skull
And cuddles the last bit of brittle from of what is left
Of his crumbling bones.

The Killer Pumpkin unrests in the dust of over-written poetry
Obsessed by ravens, mothers and sex.
Wishes he had more gravitas and chutzpah,
More sound-bites and screams.
He's getting weary, nuzzled and cosy for a good day's sleep
Before dusk descends.
He yawns and stretches, takes a bite of Twinkie,
And Vincent Price once again narrates
The God forsaken darkness of his sugar-rushed daydreams.

sometimes the sky

Some men are bullied.

sometimes the sky's too far
just too far
and you can't even reach the end of your bed
lost in blanket black holes
itch and scratch
endless folds incessant
rip at skin
you clutch
at pain so hard and so in your stomach
you're doubled
and no-one's grief could be this pain
and why would anyone grieve

you stop
gulp
dry brittle
hardly
spittle
you sob

swallowed
in
swallowing

swallowed
in
swallowing

swallowed
in
swallowing

and wish until you believe
you can make it go away
and it won't go away
it really won't
and you pray to the god who makes you grieve
to take it all away

to put it on a rocket ship and dump it
on the furthest planet's furthest sun

so they and the fear

and the lack of self respect can burn

to the nothing you are

until you are ashes

until you are dust

until you're not even a memory

and no ears can hear
and no mouths can tell
and no cars can come to your rescue
and sometimes it's tablets
and sometimes it's booze
and sometimes it's falling
and sometimes it's brutal in-between train tracks

in the lakes you've filled with tears

in the cliff faces you've carved your name
in the skin dug in
in the floor banged on
in the not knowing who you are

and why you could be so hated
and how they could behave that way
and how you believe them
and why you believe them

and how could they
make you think there is nothing
make you think you are nothing
make you want not breathing

and how you want them dead
in violent bloody revenge
and how that revenge is right
and how no-one's on your side

cold and the steel of fear
music you no longer hear
and favourite sweet
sexiest soap star
and half of E
and cider drunk
are gone in the taste of nothing
but sometimes the sky

sometimes

sometimes the sky

is something to hold on to.

Little John

Some men are foundations.
This for my nephew John Butler the Second, who is only one year younger
than me. A best friend and brother.

The love I have for you is treasure true,
Glittering piracy in the dark.
In my chest, shimmering with the very best
Of the very young of us,
The spotty.

It's wrapped up in those tapes of plays
We'd replay for my mother in our Lapworth Street bedroom.
Bray Studios of Scottie Road.
Funny voices,
Hammer Horror and very special effects.
Peter Cushing and Christopher Lee,
Brides of Dracula and The Mummy.
Our imaginations bound, soared like vampire bats.
C-30, C-60, C-90 Go!

Elvis and Doctor Who.
Patrick Troughton and The King took us through tough times.
We were fans of not joining in,
Of not starting at the beginning.
Too busy holding our families together,
Peculiar glue that gelled through the
'60s, '70, '80s, gone.

You're superhero shaped,
The time-tunnel allowing my escape,
Strength bigger and bolder than John Wayne,

Fuller than Mersey Beat.
I should've known then
You'd become a wise old sage,
Skinny framed with a cigar.

And there you are with your family,
The enigma of our Joan,
The eccentric fiddle-de-dee of David and Wesley,
Tracksuited scally.
Trouble to door troubadours,
All the cheek of comedy
Clucking Scouse cockily over broods of their own.

We're sketched deftly,
Crumbling drinking melancholy,
Mote dusting dandruff powdering our past.
The rust of good looking hard times.
Shakin' Stevens and Phil Oakey
Soundtracks respectively.

Batman and Robin had nothin' on us,
Not as quirky or witty.
Just better dressed.

The Boogie Man

Some men are dancers.

Doesn't wanna eat you and though they're sharp,
Doesn't need your flesh adorning his teeth.
He's better dressed than that,
Snappy, a dandy and a clown.
Look at his feet,
Crocodile trainers so fast in the blur you can read shine.

Hoopa doopa whey hey hey,
Surreal,
Surrender,
So real.

He tenders the world in loving arms, swinging.
Tell your children, even with fangs all men are dancers.

He's in lupine bloom, a full-blooded vampire,
One day he'll maybe dance The Frankenstein.

The Boogie Man and his legion of followers,
Who aren't his followers, know death
But they're not bothered by that right now.
The dead are lights,
Lasers.
Heart sent
And strobing.

Doesn't hang in darkness,
Doesn't illuminate it,

Just knows it's there.

Invulnerable,
Iron Man so malleable,
Working out the math holding us all together.

Tell your children The Boogie Man doesn't add up.
Tell them he's not a teacher,
He's just a glimmer of hope
With all the other glimmers of hope and sunshine.
Until he's fucked up and strung out on Monday.

Monday's child is off his face.

Air in your smile,
A "We Are Family" man,
And there really is no such thing as pain.
Huge in insensibility,
Taller than a top hat cloud,
And convinced with arms in the air we can cure the world.

There, That Bloke Under The Tree

Some men are festivals.

There, that bloke under the tree, the one writing his thoughts.
You can tell he's writing his thoughts, he has no pen.
The one who knows all men feel guilty about being men.
Dapple patterned and apple blossomed,
The man with the half smile
And sure as sixpence grin,
The one who's played chequers with queens
And lived to tall the tales.
He's got the wind on his side and feeling cheeky.

You know the one,
Rubs his hands on trees
And reads the books they'll become.
A bit dog-eared.
Cheats and peeks at the end so he knows whodunit,
Seen what the Butler's seen before the Butler even saw it.

Everybody's make believe dad, all Sid James and Doctor Who.
Works that imaginary dad vibe like a gigolo.
Fisherman cool,
Hot-pants and waders,
Shouts and whispers.
Hipsters.

Does a belting Tommy Cooper,
Kicks five footballs and keeps them
And eleven best friends in the air,
On his head, off his head, and goal.

His feet tap in time to the earth,
So fast he looks footless,
Fancy free, and with the wind in what's left of his hair
Hums the one about mice
And the inquisitive tin-whistle.
Animated like childhood telly,
Singing,
Ringing.

There he is, there.
The one who makes circles with corners
And rooms without walls.
Stretches time like elastic,
Sketches space,
Doors wide open,
Overflowing whisky and tea
And a running buffet that's finished a Marathon.

Has a joke for every tear,
One photo of every season of every year.

Sharp witted Raggedy-Dan,
Hat has tendrils,
Soft focused feel-good fool.
And, although he's engraved his own headstone
And will be at his own funeral,
He'll never die.

Got clouds sewn up in rainbow thread and ribbons,
Like a robin in and out of thunderstorms.
Rain dot to dots the world, doesn't bother joining them.
Won't see the point in lines, "They picket fence truth",
And don't get him going on lies.

He'll only tell you,
"Lies are more human, far more human than truth ever could be."
Be careful listening,
He'll insist truth can never really be written down.

You know the one.
Knows only babies laugh honestly
And women know more than they're letting on,
That the way we live now was the blueprint for the Titanic.
Don't panic! Don't panic!
Generous as a nervous breakdown.

Gets away with the murder he wants to commit,
The deaths he deftly imagines.

You know who I mean,
He's so done it all.
Kids the zeitgeist it's onto a winner.
Marvels at the way tattoos look similar
And illustrate the same story,
Willow Pattern skin.

He thinks clothes are words on bodies, misspelt,
And he's got this feeling.

I saw him once before under that tree
Writing a letter to America and his arm went mental.
A bit Jon Pertwee and exploding watch,
A bit frilly shirt and apocalypse,
A bit Mr God from Dulwich,
As he signed his name Bob
With cryptic agility and an undeniably avant-garde flourish.

And Then The Man Said

Some men are mythical trips through story-telling.

I looked to the water like it could answer in waves.
It skimmed questions like scallies throwing stones.
"Stones and water," the man said,
"Believe me, you can't live without them.
Watch the stones sink. See!
Free, like they're flying.
Sinking like the first time they've flown."

The man speaks in a cow-bell riddle.
His voice cuts through,
An ancient hot knife slicing the butter of souls.
The man's on a roll, reverberating,
Watch him go, the flow carrying that barrel
All the way down Niagara.

When she stopped pouting, Monroe knew the man.
Held her like candyfloss that could split the atom.
Told her all men were not the same,
That some men are truly animals.
Honest,
Hungry and protecting.
Some men are a bitch wolf, a baby seal,
Some men are the rush of forest between paws.
"Can you imagine the scent?"
Monroe always knew the potential of men.

"What else did the man say?" asked the crossed legged child,
Begging stories.

The man said,
"Find a safe space, negotiate friendship
Without language or money,
And dance, kid, like you could lift from the floor.
Go tell the stars a thing or two.
Tell them they don't have the monopoly on shining
And don't forget to dance with them.
That's what they want, waiting to be asked,
Exited shy.
Why else they twinkle so bashful?"

He said,
"I'm a woman son,"
To the child he left behind.
"I'm every woman."

He said,
"Find the singer who opens your heart and tell them.
Tell them they're everything, that they are gods, truly gods.
Tell them it's their voices that grasp eternity and fill you with
Moments of faith.
Tell them,
Tell them good, real good.
Then they'll know heaven.
Singers deserve this,
They're like children.
Why else would they sing?"

He said,
"You can't teach compassion.
You must show it."

And then the man said,

"I might have lied,
But I hope in glorious Technicolor."

The man died before he was born.
No sexy nurse could pamper him.
He never got to know the word Paparazzi.
He couldn't even try to be the perfect man.
Cut short before he could grow.
He was too dangerous, could've won the war,
But would not have fought.
Instead, he sits, calm,
Languid sometimes, waiting,
In the absolute what might have been of men.

Love Those Frankenstein Guys

Some men are drunks.

Thickset
Home to a mumble,
Incoherent under booze and slap-dash
They'll buy you a pint and don't want one back.
You're their oldest friend, long as the night is young,
So many stories made of imbecile dribblings,
Full of eloquent apology,
No-one's more sorry.
Shaped by urgency not remembered,
Often wonder whose head they're wearing.

Ever seen a face home to a beating and a smile?

Pulled apart by life,
Held together by their own stitching,
Songs, a kick and punch of melody.
Bruised,
Melancholy blued,
Battered and sometimes left for dead.
Been dads,
More than one kid,
A bride in every pint, a story in every port.
Out of control,
There's no punctuation in beer.
Some of them doctors,
Some of them queer.
Can't remember their last hard on,
Forgetting forgotten.

The times I've spent with them.
Good times.

Those Frankenstein guys
Have no idea they've been made.
The only way was a dead end.
That the bottle would be a natural home,
A châteaux
Cut off from the beast of reality,
Living lives where White Lightening often strikes twice.

I've watched them cry into their beer,
Very real tears,
Sobbing about opportunities missed or cocked up.
Seen them thrown out of pubs for being too destroyed.

I love their wisdom and finality.
Shivering fragility.
Chest rattle after every joke,
And belief in a god who has long forsaken them.

They belong drunk.

The night would not be the same,
They're its realities.
Hallucinating dancers illuminating the street,
Accompanied by show tunes long forgotten.
Lumbering home,
Limbs not theirs,
Jig of life and dearth.
Wing and prayer hopeful bed will cushion their fall.

Spending a fortune and lifetime dead to the world.

The Ballad Of Jimmy Butler

Some men are stories smoked in the corners of pubs.
Jimmy Butler was my dad. He left my mother and her family when she
was four months pregnant with me. He broke my mother's heart. All
my childhood he was an enigma. I saw him maybe twice, no more. He
was a man. He died and became legend. Ordinary, fascinating and
unfulfilling, but if anyone deserves a ballad it's him. After he died I
hooked up with some of his friends and his delicious concubine, Dixie,
in The Liverpool, a pub near the Pier Head. This is a patchwork of my
relationship with him, her, and that night. "Stay-behind" is Scouse
for an after hours lock-in.

I'll iron out the parchment,
Reconfigure the hieroglyphics,
Ancient out the rough spots
With a tear so old it's run out of ink.

I don't catch myself blaming anymore,
I don't catch my breath.

You're old Jimmy Butler.
You always were.

"Gerard, your dad's nothin' but a dirty rotten filthy stinkin'
    whore master."
My mother's name for you,
The first words I remember.
No wonder I'm a poet.
So, I'll write a ballad. The ballad of a bad lad
Who could carry a tune,
A ballad of a bad lad who could whisper to mules.

I love that war story, my dad the mule whisperer.
You didn't drive trains, you weren't a spy,
A Spitfire Jimmy Stewart dog-fighting, a God blessed America.
You had the power to commune with beasts,
Only The Chosen can do that.
I imagine the blood, mud and terror.
Our Chris tells me you never talked about it.
"A dirty rotten filthy stinkin' whore master."

This isn't about leaving,
Abandonment.
It's about singing in that pub with Dixie.
You'd been dead a year,
I'd carried your coffin.
Weirdest thing I ever did.
Ghost kid.

It was an old man's pub.
The scent of dusk and lager.
Dixie shone,
A Goddess of men who paid at her altar.
"Your Jimmy Butler's lad," she said.
Her voice Scouse raucous,
Her cleavage boasting conquests.
Gorgeous.
"Yes."

In the drunk of her memories, we sang.
I know the songs, not the words.
Dixie whisks me in the chorus of her bosom.
She makes me you, a whore whisperer.
And it turns
The night,

It swirls.

She says,
"Nobody will love ye like a nobody can love ye."
Weeps and cheers.
"Your dad was a good man with a great voice.
A singer with the whole room in mind."
Dixie showed me the romantic, the gypsy,
The man she loved.
The lover.
Her fellah,
The man who got the whole pub singing.
I imagine the blood, mud and terror.
You never mentioned the war.
Dixie told me I was just like you.

So, I'll sing a ballad, a ballad of Jimmy Butler.
Bald hustler,
Ribald bluster, a quiet man,
Seller of a good time.
Of the dad I never knew and whose songs I sang
And followed in the dance steps of.
Woman lover,
Heart breaker,
Whore master,
Mule whisperer,
The history of a no-one loved by a pub.
A heartbeat of Liverpool,
Griever,
The docker and ship's scaler,
Army man, reluctant sailor
And legend in his own stay behind.

Comrade Brother

Some men are irreplaceable.
This is about being a kid and having older brothers in the sixties, seventies
and eighties. Some of them have since died. It is dedicated to my dear friend
Fas and inspired by his brother, Michael Farrell. A Class Warrior.

Great big shapes,
Solid blunderers,
Builders that hug, thug, protect.
Run rings round you with nifty footwork,
Rough and tumble, purple and blue.
But big brothers are more colours than that, they're the
Seasons of your childhood,
Football strips
And Captain Scarlet.

My brothers had fists and mouths a-plenty,
Loud at night,
Stealthy.
Solid as shadows in the front yard, down the back entry
Scruffians before they were dandies.

The reason bonfire nights blazed.
Treasonable as gunpowder plots,
Sparky.
Threw bangers and Roman Candles in the air,
Turned me and the time to fireworks.
They smell of burning,
Chips, kissing girls,
Smoking and sagging school.
Smell exiting as crime.

Cavemen.
Scrape you cross the pavement and hang you over the landing.
If you cry, do it more.
Ghost noises behind the door.
On the back of a bike whooping at speed,
On the corner looking out for police.
Brothers teach you what's right,
How to spit and whistle,
Fart well,
The anarchy of swearing;
Currency when you're a kid.
The lessons you shouldn't teach.
Night scented stocky.
All the fun of the fear,
Loads cleverer than skool.

Brutal in Kes, sat at prayer in The Last Supper.

They pocket money,
Send you straight the shop.
Want ciggies, razors and some of your sweets.
You get this feeling they love being older
And you need them to be older,
Even when they make you cry.
They love it when you hate them.
Bastards love it when they make you cry.

Brothers go to work and come back dirty-hungry,
Eat plates of food you couldn't climb the south face of.
Laugh about bosses,
Hug their mates.
At weekends stink of Old Spice.
My brothers looked like footballers at weekends.

Not on the pitch, in the magazines.
The George Best end of magazines,
Eventually evolving into Kevin Keegan
And the great smell of Brut.

They fight drunken,
Sometimes each other.
White shirt, black eye and still get the girls.
And still get them pregnant.
They're amazing!
All these things and so much more,
Do all the things you can't,
But all the things you're born for.
At night they even get the bus into town.
Brothers are exotic.

Brothers cry
Unforgettable tears.
Know when one of them is missing.

Bashed

Some men are violent.
A true story, one of the very few downsides of 1980.

Easy to recall this,
not stored away with the dust sheets and unmemorable
with the ooh-la-la and unmentionable,
the oopsy daisy and lamentable.
Still as vivid as the first episode of *Rock Follies*
but there's no musical number,
no escape in it,
song 'n' dance.
No chance to meet Julie Covington,
call her a genius and duet with it.

You romanced yourself a boxer
and boy you were a bruiser.
I remember the thrill of your muscles,
the super scally skill of your hustles,
the way you sang "Geno" all dead Dexy on yourself,
dead sexy.

Everyone's taken a long time telling me
you're what a real man should be.
Remember you grabbing my shoulders,
hugging and saying you'd protect me.
Your voice a fighting and comforting Scouse,
familiar as my brothers'.
You were one of the good blokes,
not camp bitchy like the others.
A strawberry blonde whose jaw could crack nuts easy as jokes.

You'd bought me drinks and took me from Sadie's,
that night club with so many memories.
The one with the just released queens,
taxi drivers, trannies and intellectual whores
that felt and smelt like The Cantina from *Star Wars*.
You'd sniffed poppers and danced with me, told me I was
pretty and you'd fuck me like a girl.
Didn't wanna be your girl but I pretended to be defenceless,
so much glorious pretending,
relentless.
So much was about the swirl of those moments in your arms
and your low down dog-rough dirty charms.

The alley outside
Santa-Monica Boulevard,
Liverpool Berlin and well 'ard.
You were Brad Davis *Querelle*-ing me.
You were so protecting and you got me so pretending,
got me so I couldn't see.
I fell in teenage with you, the night and debauchery.

Tell me your muscles are for me,
I hang off your arm like a handbag.
Your lips are for me,
I'm on your mouth like a whisper,
and the hard on you're boasting,
the hard on I'm groping, is for me,
that I'm a lucky little girl.
Not arsed being your girl, just want you naked.
Even kiss me outside the chippy,
Lit emerald green and married.

The salt and vinegar walk to my house

is a film with Audrey Hepburn,
Moon River Mersey, wide as your smile.
Every step and chip a delicious condiment of destiny,
George Peppard and Holly Golitely,
Breakfast at Gerry's.

At home you're sweating,
I ask you if you're all right.
Say you need a cup of tea,
say your head's bangin' and you need the toilet for a wee.
Order me to take off my clothes, cheeky chapilly.
I bin what's left of the chips from the chippy,
disrobe eagerly.
I just want the musk of porn and Disney,
The King and I and "Shall We Dance" with Jeff Stryker agility.

The lights go out,
puzzles me,
know there's more than enough money in the leccy,
it must be a power cut,
then door off its hinges and
BAM!

The tumble and bang of my cheek on the floor the roar of your
voice raging Queer! The weight of your body pounding my
skin your hand on my mouth and Queer! The white flash in
my head as you punch my face the stunned of the heat of your
rage. The panic of sound and blubber of voice the thud of my
body and wall. The kick in the gut and lack of sound the spin
of body and wall no pain then crack then pain and punched
no pain then back on the floor. The bellow of money you want
my money the butt to the head the crack of bone then bang my
head on the floor. Pain then no pain the blubber of "Please!"

the rush to the cupboard drawer the throwing of money the punch of face the hit of table and sprawl. The shatter of glass of hope and illusion the kick in the head then stars. The panic the screams the grab of throat the rape of lips the push the thud the wall. Pinned to the wall and the promise of death the spit of death the laugh at my naked form. Your face so close your rage so close your death shoved down my throat. You tell me I'm dead you promise my death no pain then white then flash then white the wall. It's like I'm not here it's like I'm no-one at all no-one at all no-one at all no-one at all the sound of my begging then the wall sound of my begging then the wall sound of my begging then the wall then the wall sound of my begging then the wall sound of my begging then the wall then the wall sound of my begging then the wall sound of my begging then the wall.

Fall.

Laugh.

Floor.

Like I'm no-one at all.

Tell me you're going to kill me.

Sound of my begging.

Really believe I will die.

Sound of my begging.

Cover myself with the *TV Times*.

Stop, laugh and ask, "Where's my jewellery."

Somewhen

Some men are gay.

Somewhen, someone once sung,
"Somewhere Over the Rainbow".
A childish plea for a Technicolor dawn,
Bluebirds flying and a playtime of rest.

There, like lemon-drops and chimney tops,
We'd fade marsh-mallow curls and angel delights
Into dancefloors, alive with the underground
Thunder-thump sweaty of Oz.
Emerald queens.
I've no doubt Munchkins pinched our arses and groped our tits
But they were teenage arses and teenage tits,
Teenage Munchkins some of them,
And we'd've been fumin' if they hadn't.

That same song found a tear we all could cry,
Schmaltz with pain and just the right overhang of longing.
It sits like tatty furniture, refusing to be antique.
Queen Anne with million dollar legs.
In some gay's wildest dream
Betty Grable "owns" that song.
In some gay's wildest dream
Kylie "owns" that song.
In some gay's wildest dreams there's
Somewhen.

Then, after the war
And disco devastation,

The blood-curdling weep of grief
And techno.
After the battlefields of loss and cruising,
Poppers sniffed to remember our dead,
That song somehow still rings.
Sings
A lament of billowing promise,
Of footsteps taken,
Of paths trodden.
In drag,
In fury,
In gingham.
Always in Judy and in glorious black and white.

A Statue To See-Anne

Some men are not just men.
There are so many statues in our country, icons to oppression and slavery. We
have a huge statue of Queen Victoria in Liverpool. A statue infamously
famous for the size of her penis. It's my dream to replace it with a very
modern icon. My old friend Shaun/See-Anne has been queen of Liverpool for
most of his/her forty five years. Riah is an ancient gay word for hair. Listen up
you daffodils, this is written in Scouse.

Y'gonna need a lorra stuff.
Mix the bronzer with showbiz an' rhythm
An' stir it universal clockwise.
Find a cast bold enough to hold it an' let it set
In the unsettlin' sons of Mother Mersey.
Solid as the colour of sunrays,
Hard as man.
She's a golden horizon wigglin' with stiletto blur,
Walkin' on water from Birkenhead
To the Liver Birds.

Give her wings and rest,
Angel and eiderdown.
She deserves to fly.
Watch her weft her way round rain,
Makin' a riah from clouds.
Blonde an' candyfloss,
Sassy an' well boss,
Goddess for the dancin' class.
More stories than an ocean full o' sailors.
More balls than a city full o' gangsters.
Brass.

An' you'll need iron for this
Sheffield steel.
Make her stainless, nothin' sticks.
Make sure Cammell Laird's docked up on glitter,
She must shine before settin' sail.
This girl's Titanic,
Unsinkable.
Original,
Unthinkable.
An invisible man,
Unmissable.
An' who else could do it?

Pull down Victoria an' her dirty past,
Clean the street,
Find the shine; she never made the city sway,
She never rainbow eyed.
An' in her place erect a statue to See-Anne,
Androgynine.
She's Princess Road.
Gritty royalty,
Pretty.
Lookin' like she loves,
Like she's laughin',
Lookin' likes she's dancin'.
"Are ye askin'?"
Lookin' like she knows how to unslave a world.

A Little Bag Of Sad

Some men want to be women.

And, in a little bag of sad
All of Pandora's woes and worries
Stands at the hem of his lady,
Uninvolved, unloved,
At the mercy of her stitching and biology.
He's a lipstick smear,
Embroidered and embroiled
In the stockings and suspense of her legacy.
He stares at the mirror.
She half-smiles like Diana Dors.
Smoke-trail her signature,
A half-pout name tangible as vapour.

In the aisles of Sainsbury's,
Thinks as her,
Mutters as her,
Fumbling beans and mayonnaise.
He's not dressed as her,
Pandora must never be seen.
She beguiles behind fans,
Hides behind excuses.
Red satin denial,
Lacey knickered whispers,
Racy and misconstrued.

In the pub, drowning in football,
Goals scored and the roar of conquests mounted,
Sits in his silence.

And in his silence, sits in what other women wear.
His wife gin tonics, glistens in the earrings he bought.
She trinkets on and on of their daughters' desires to be women,
"Just dressing up, still little girls, Geoff."

Death, Me And A Taxi

Some men are very frightened.

I wish the lines on my face were winding roads to wisdom,
Finding caves of hermits contemplating words I wove carelessly,
Words I threw away because dancing turned my hand to catapults.
I've seen my best work slide down nightclub walls
Next to the go-go,
Gone on the twist,
Shook on the hip,
Shot from the glass.
I once saw my words on a mirror-ball.
The best thing I ever saw.

Then it's Death and me in a cab,
Someone I picked up because the dancing stopped.
Asked for a cigarette to calm his blues,
His bird did some jigging with some bad news.
Felt sorry for his fingers shakin',
Sovereigns a-rattlin' on his bones.
He got sick,
Threw up the anger of his youth
And in the bile I could see his golden moments.
Death was a nice kid,
His art tossed aside because he was too good at football.
Wanted to be sensitive and draw sound around flowers.

The taxi driver shouts,
Death and me get out.
I ask him up for coffee,

Says he's not ready.
Assure him I ain't looking for commitment,
Tells me he's freaked.
There's grovelling apology
And grabs a cab back to town.

Seems the lines on my face were the road home
And I'm the hermit,
Picking words off mirror-balls,
Placing poetics,
Meaning
And little squares of glass
On Death's side of the bed.

Jimmy Bling

Some men are scallies.

With a Rockport heart Jimmy Bling's kicking back
With every bit of coke and crack eroded and stuck up his nose.
A two finger pose struck at those who suppose
Everything he knows is shit.
Jimmy's a dead-end kid blistered by the fists
Of drunks who baby-sit their sons and daughters,
Telling bedtime stories of prison-hits, page three tits
And the purity of skag.

Jimmy's been a bag-head,
A soggy slow-mo drag-head, pushing aside his pain.
Trading abuse for contraband,
Swapping tricks with a sleight of hand
Even magicians couldn't see.
Too many blind eyes and half-thoughts,
Wars declared and unfought,
Too many roars coloured in the passion of anecdotal destiny.

In the grey brick hell of Her Majesty's cell,
After night-sweats and horrors,
After the fights and bothers of Her Majesty's brothers,
Calling shots and shooting pool,
After the fool-jerk talk of making money
And the dreams of sunny-sides
And pussy-hunny,
Jimmy Bling rewrites the rules.

Yeah, Jimmy Bling's fighting back

With a head full of Pink Floyd and Eminem,
With the scream of a warrior everyman,
With the beat-fire of streets embedded in his soul.
Jimmy Bling feels whole and raging,
His mind-knuckles engaging a punchbag symmetry.
Has a society cemetery where dead-heads
He's never tried to impress
Rest in the inconsistency of their rules and deregulations.
Jimmy Bling's ringing in the congratulations
Of knowing exactly who he and the enemy is.
He's got it sussed,
It really is Them and Us,
Pure as lust, distant as love,
Gloves off and furious.
No ifs, no butts,
Just blood-words and word-guts.

Jimmy Bling's found museums and galleries,
Revels in the parodies artists see,
Immersed in brush strokes and philosophy,
Impressed by the metals of weaponry
And futility and necessity of war.
Stumbled across poetry, fell in love with poetry,
Wrote "Gentle" for his sister Tiffany
And performed it at his local bar.
It's the first time he's really heard applause,
First time he's really been endorsed,
First time he saw what the middle-class see.

Jimmy Bling's fighting back
With a belly of fire and a diamond tongue,
Singing songs unsung by his sister.
Finally his own mister

With a head full o' rhymes, a net full o' goals.
And to the joy of fools and scholars
Jimmy Bling hollers
His raps and heart-felt scorn.
Jimmy Bling's reborn
With tales of skag-head porn and the comedy of shit telly
In the cata-wombs of a city's underbelly,
A pulse of the ne'er-do-wells and never-ready
In the dark of boho dawn.

Knows he's hit his "Ting!"
The crowd sing:
Jimmy Bling,
Jimmy Bling,
Jimmy Bling.

The Shmuck

Some men are really very human.

The Shmuck's bought new clothes.
Shoes.
Wants to look casual yet smart.
Dreams of a fast car and being a boy racer
With Bobby Horrop from senior school.
Dreams about Speedos,
Needing and streamlined reflections.

He really believes in the world around him, in hope
And a two point four by four family.
Likes Sarah and Robert as names.
Decides not to wear a tie.

Looks in the mirror.
His maroon shirt crushed velveteen.

In the mirror,
The Shmuck triple chins and stomachs
His way through practised chat up lines.
Talks of sci-fi and politics.
Spits a little,
Says he's a feminist.
Fluent in Klingon.
Knows there's a Mrs Shmuck somewhere
Dying to know his trivia.

Mrs Shmuck won't come out of hiding.
Maybe she's alien.

He jokes about her wearing a cloaking device.
He enjoys the bitter memories of school.
They nicknamed him Donut.
Sweet.
At least they knew he was there.

Going to a club tonight,
Calls it a disco.
A singles night he found online,
Spelt S.I.N.G.L.Z.Z.Z., it's sci-fi themed.
Maybe Mrs Shmuck will be there
Dressed like Seven of Nine in sequins.
If they play "Echo Beach" he'll dance.
The Shmuck's got rhythm.

First he'll go to Café Hollywood
And sit through beans on toast
With a promise of two desserts on his lips.
Marilyn Monroe is almost even,
James Dean crooked.
David Niven looks quizzically on.

A potential Mrs Shmuck used to work there.
He read her name:
Julie.
Julie Shmuck... he dreamt.
Went to see her line dance.
Bought her a drink,
Was laughing too hard when he gave it her,
All his teeth and gums
Gingivitis and orange.
He'll get a little of his two spotted dicks on his shirt.
Crushed velveteen.

He's exited by the night and a slightly drunken kebab.
At forty-four, still feels the overspill of teenageing.
Says he's an optimist.
Be home by twelve-thirty,
Splattered a little with rejection and chilli sauce.
"It'll keep what's left of the spotted dicks
Company."

Turns the key.
Tunes into a DVD.

Stuck into Ben and Jerry's
As Captain Janeway,
Bikinied,
Whispers sweet nothings on a holodeck of a dessert island.

Community Of One

Some men find themselves alone.

Barbed wine in a community of one,
Jagged and sharp,
A spiky garland of fuck ups and pin-pricks
Scarring a broken history red,
Like a kind rapist burning his fingers for charity
And declaring tabloid love for *The Sun.*

Open heart in a lion's mouth,
Pulsing,
Roaring regret
And
Apology.

There's an old sap in a thunder cloud
Carving pithy and selfish figures.
Places them on the ground where they degrade,
Unctuous sullen,
Into bleached barren earth.

A walk through a breakdown,
Nervous,
And feet are shocking, shaky,
Painful.
The scenery spits dreadfuls
And wilds
Out of control.
It dissolves hairy into unforgiving fissures.

The shelter of yesterdays
Vanish
And he's left with cold unhurried
Calm.
Friends are wonderful.
He's wished the best possible lager through his sorrow.

Men In The Ink

Some men are depressed.

All in it together, black as pitch people
Blanched and bedraggled in the motionless sky,
No star-shine ricochet reflecting handsomely off our eyes.

Wet in Hell.
Antichrist is all out of fire.
He breezes nonsense on petrified demons who have long
Relinquished their impishness.

Satan's tired of tears,
Steam bubbling off cheeks.

All hope inane and the street theatre banners read "lost".
It's scraggy agitprop, boneless,
Out of breath and meaning.

It's hard to ignite a revolution in Hades these days.

Swimless in filth, reeking in our gut, making wretched our speech.
Words are puddles pissed in by dogs,
Vomited by drunks.

Weights of fists pummel the only brute force we can muster.
The boxer in us is getting his own back,
Wants to see how much more we can take.

Satan strikes a cigarette, the match stutters defeat.
Soggy sulphur splutters, spitting off and on neon.

Satan punches the boxer, blackens his eye.
Hell is hello written in blood,
Dried black, a crimson dust goodbye.

Lonely Seeks Moonbeam

Some men will kill being shy.

Stuck in a desert taking tea with the sand,
Holding out a sugar-bowl to a mirage.
"One lump or two?"
At home here, in a space big enough
To be small enough for one.
Tells a joke to a flower gasping for water,
Gasping for water 'cos it doesn't take tea.
The lonely man looks to the sun,
Wide-eyed and hopeful it'll blind him,
Burn out his eyes.
Doesn't want to see a world refusing.
Can't make head nor tail of the horror of decisions.
Er, um.
The lonely man's searching,
Eyes burning,
Searching for a moonbeam to carry him away.

His mother called him shy,
Apologised for his silence.
His father kicked a ball, it hit him in the head.

Has an apartment on Jupiter,
A duplex for him and the aliens.
He's happy to wait three billion years before they call.
There's enough tea to quench a planet,
Enough milk to last eternity,
Ammunition to slaughter a village.
He's waiting for someone to invent the eternal biscuit

He can buy off eBay.
He's confident on eBay.
He can order high pitched and slow-mo,
Cake shops a no-go.
Voices!
Hates punching the dark before they talk.
Voices that say,
"Come on sunshine, you'll never fit in,
Your laugh is fake and they all know you're lying."
The only voices he owns the names of.
They're an audience booing his successes.
Point out his bald patch when he bows.

The man behind the desk:
"Do you have a partner?"
Repeated:
"Do you have a partner?"

Walks to the post office
And people are effects,
Strobing in colours,
Whining in sound.
They pass him with a breeze.
He's found himself on the floor before now,
Gasping and talking to cracks.
Cracks laughing at his pathetic attempts at conversation.
He once took a crack home.
Introduced it to the desert,
Told it about the aliens,
Tried to kiss and feel its arse.
The crack laughed at the size of his dick
And insisted on a cup of tea.
"One lump or two?"

Tried to book a holiday.
The smiling woman smiled even wider.
Asked his destination.

Tiny Bangs

Some men can't run from, or talk about, their feelings.

You know you're a higgledy-piggaldy thing
When upside-down seems sideways on.
Like it's coming at you from a time-trail
Zooming the other way forward.
When the reasons for one thing are out-weighed
And bullied by another
And no one decision is rich in validity or choice.
You're this constant collusion of wrong and right
And a pile-up of crunching achievement.
There you are on the motorway of life,
Mangled as mince, politely passing the time of day.
You say to the car crash:
"How goes your business, tea-lights still selling well, are they?"
And a stretched taut, agony rippled, face replies:
"The bottom fell out of tea-lights some time ago mate,
Into computers now, selling futures to people
Trying to forget their past."
You nod politely as a broken neck allows,
Genuinely feel sorry for the demise of the tea-light and reply:
"Well, let's hope to high heaven the bottom doesn't fall out of
    futures."

Sometimes you're sat at a desk
Or at home
Enjoying the melody of a cup of tea and memories,
When a whoever, dressed in whatever,
Bursts down the door and insists it's
"THE END OF THE WORLD!"
Such a brawl and yell it puts you off your sip.

Then, there's the "Can I be bothered panicking?
It's only the end of the world",
Because you were told so many times
There were so many worlds for you,
Losing this one is a piece of piss.
Sometimes you like this world,
Really understand fresh air,
Conversation and ice cream,
And wish the gibbering man would put a sock in it.
Sometimes you couldn't agree with the gibbering man more.

Ever sat in a cemetery enjoying the screwy of squirrels
And their constant dance of food,
When, would you Adam and Steve it, a bomb explodes?
I haven't, but sometimes feel like it has.
It's a tiny bang and it's inside.
No-one sees the rip and shreds
Or your flesh fruiting the trees.
And, although your limbs are strewn all over the place,
You can still walk to the bank and sign cheques.
You can still pour milk on cornflakes.
You can still laugh, so you must be alright.
You can order a table for two,
Buy flowers awash with subtlety and fragrance,
And demand a few hours from a whore.
You can sit with that whore for some time.
You can even listen.
And the whore's conversation is punctuated,
As is your conversation,
By love,
Intrusion,
Apology,
And tiny bangs.

The Quiet Place

Some men have no idea of silence.

Where strings of promise unwind
Tendrils of touchy-feely grace are threatened.
Here, the men in the quiet place set sail their dreams,
Encased in blossom and thorn, they sleep.

They cage sorry in skin of lips, in cave of teeth,
To be let out when ears are gone.
Sorry knows no freedom in the quiet place.

The knuckles of years,
Thud of bone on bone.

Door to door,
Ring the bell of memories.
In the quiet place,
Red eyes
Weep for bruises.
They wish for faces not broken, for hearts mended,
And a mattress filled with kisses to cushion falls.
It's where poetry beaten may land,
Soft as a summer rhyme,
Gentle as a spring song.
Lyrics flighty are weighty in this wrestling noise.

The quiet place
Throbs hollow and loud its stories.
Men yell for the power of words
And the end of blood and thunder,

Yell at yells fading to echoes,
Head-butt shadows for being more real,
Black-blue their foreheads.
It's where men exhausted take leave of men and story-telling.

The blossom floating turns to birds sweeping,
Rooks, picking from pits of eyes.
A raw caw of bleeding
Cries
Unworthy.
It's bleak, harsh,
Stormy.

Where everything ever said is wrong
And bawls and pounds forever
In thought and secrets.

How Do You Respect Fuck All?

Some men riot.

Let me tell you what fuck all is.
It's invisible, nada, it's you don't exist or matter,
That's what fuck all is.
It's Theresa May, plastic-faced, spouting nothing tangible,
That's fuck all.
Fuck all is the offer on the table,
It's the option of government.
Fuck all is the Big Society,
That's fuck all.
Fuck all would spit in your eye
If it recognised your eye,
If it recognised your humanity.
Fuck all pisses all over the crap of you,
That's fuck all.
Fuck all is the BBC bullying Darcus Howe,
It's the BBC calling him a rioter.
The BBC, that's fuck all.
Fuck all ignores the question,
It hides in denial.
Fuck all loves us blaming,
That's fuck all.
Fuck all takes your jobs,
Your libraries,
Your hospitals,
Your pubs,
Bulldozes your youth clubs,
Labels you lazy and nothing,
That's fuck all.

Fuck all destroys more than we burn,
It's the politics of the rich and evil.
And, yes, I said evil.
A tramp dies of cold
In the shadow of an empty home,
That's fuck all.
That's evil.

People are fuck all.
Poor people are fuck all,
Angry people are fuck all,
Addicts are fuck all,
Students are fuck all,
The unemployed are fuck all,
The dispossessed are fuck all,
The unemployable are fuck all,
Single mothers are fuck all,
The unlovable are fuck all,
The mentally ill are fuck all,
The abused are fuck all,
The fucked are fuck all.

Fuck all will burn down your capital,
That's fuck all.

Betting

Some men gamble.

In the betting of reality, big people fall,
Bang their heads and nurse lumps of ego goo.
It's a big life,
Betting.
Sweatin' on legs eleven,
Waiting for a mansion to call
"House!"
All the big people dwarfed by the shadow of
Winning.

The betting of reality calls time on losers,
Tells them:
"Push off will ye kids, I've a tarantula to cuddle
And haven't the time for
Sunday dinner decisions
Augmented as it were by the gravy of tears.
You've gorra look out for yer'selves now.
The war is over."
The betting of reality shouts
"Bingo!",
Slaps the face of his kids
Wanting a hug and a packet of crisps.

It's in the betting of all things
We trust,
The Bingo of all wings.
It's in the thrust of the Big Bang,
The curious logic of motion.

I've seen council estates mimic
Its centrifugal grace,
Seen them be the definition of
Pop-up.

Betting strangleholds the intellect of politics with
Mickey Mouse machinations.
Betting misbehaves,
Shits its pants
So at least it can stink.
Betting tells you "I'm here!",
It's not afraid of stinking.
Bad betting and the ballad of pungent altruism,
The spark of vodka and coke twinkles in its eyes,
A black and gold agenda,
Drowning.

Betting's a coke-head president
With a battlefield of experience to inject.
Betting triumphs when all else
Fails.
Trailblazes a poppycock camp
Of truisms
And balls.

Betting millionaires the unworthy
And whispers victims to rippers.
Try sipping a cuppa tea with it without shaking.
Go on, I dare you.
Only cockroaches and betting will survive a nuclear assault.

Within the myriad of questioning
Betting dances the answers,

Pogoing in the tell-tale gossip of mothers,
Laughs at the ambitions of socialism.
It's in the protocols of computers imitating information.
Betting, a savage teenager preferring a suit to safety-pins.
Betting rattles along
At a fair lick,
Rollin'
A
Rock.
Rattlin'
A
Brick.

In A Liverpool Moment

Some men are cities.

Written in glaciers,
Parables encased in north wind whispers.
It reads: "Blood in the sea, blood in the vein."
It rawks the hulls of the invincible
Like a laugh ripping through a wake.
In God it trusts and dodges the rent.
Boasts wicked truth in the most cruel jokes
And the
BLAM! SPLAT! POW! of their punchlines.

Not only poets see the lyrics in its industry;
Ask the wasted and jailed,
They hum in sing-song the tune of its decay.
Black as the fifties,
Tar and pitch.
A violent playground,
Colour-sound pouring like hymns
Through stained glass windows.

The filterless smoke of Woodbines;
Batons
Loose in the mouths of Marxists
Gobbing off with faith of atheists.
They booze in the company of the aged
With accordions, harmonicas,
Orchestrating a blueprint for the world.

God walked out on everybody.

Bastard!
A bad bet in too much debt.

It had too many widows and lilies,
Too many drunks alone after marriage
And more than enough circle games.

It's froth,
The suds of my mother's wash-house stories.
Worried knuckles tap the Morse-code of her grief.
She's still kind of alive in Liverpool
With the sons she buried and scolded.
The brick of football beats,
Boom-boom, boom-boom, boom-boom,
The thump of dead scallies never giving up the ghost.
I remember the arrogance of working men,
Vivid and derelict,
Torched as its warehouses,
Dancing as its discotechs.

Judy Garland pissed in The Grafton
And Pat Phoenix wore the crown.

It holds the desolate in a state of disgrace,
Canonizes fist raging men; they are the saints of sin.
Hard girls touch you up at the back of Mass.

The never erosion of the Mersey,
Lapping up wisdom in fortune cookies,
Where the world held its breath and promises.
The Chinese, most silent of its riots.

Teresa and Bunny King, glamorous baby-sitters,

Catholic as their accents, red as Rita Hayworth.
They swung high on rope from a fourth floor arch.
You could see their knickers and socks,
Hear liberation in their screams.

A stolen car in Smack-Head Street burns like a candle at a vigil,
Cold hands swarm confidently on its flames,
Stories are exchanged about how easy it is to rob the docks.

Rotten in The Curzon, five-thirty Thursday afternoon,
Other pubs are shut.
The millionaire's in trumpeting money and Champagne,
The sound of screeching,
Chorale.
Half-cut queens
Full of poppers, Bananarama
And sex.

There's a graffiti of rent boys who keep taking the tablets.
"Thou shalt boogy and boogying must be done."
Parting waves on the dancefloor, all out at sea.

And the buildings of this city
Have such wide heads and shoulders,
Shadows cast a dark embrace.
Giant bouncers huddle in concrete,
Protecting the innocence of the guilty.

Don't I say it?
Does it die?
Does the majesty of the underclass
Lie wriggling like a fish out of water,
Like a fishwife out of bread?

Folly Butler And Her Bad Man Blues

Some men are not nice.
Folly Butler is a recurring muse-like character I often write about. Each time she's a blank canvas, so anything could happen. She could be anyone or anything. There is one constant though... she can speak daffodil.

She sits soggy in the slobber of his dribbled smile,
Wretched as one of his promises,
Damp as bed-sit miserable.
He says one day he'll buy her diamonds
So she can shine like a torch through a London pea-souper.
He's got a fog-horn voice,
Baleful as Dickens's dead.
Thinks she'd be better off without him,
There's better places to sleep than doorways.
He bubbles sentences,
"I luv ye babe. Top one luv."
It swallows her senses,
The froth off scum.

He's got the benefits she's been mental enough to achieve,
Exchanges them for vodka, then sherry, then cider.
Blues her with Olympian fists,
Bruises down the word cunt till she's soaked
In his swearing and spit.
Tired of his lashings,
His rum sodomy.

She's forgotten how to swim against the tide,
How to sing in daffodil.
Mumbles about babies and the horror of war,
Mumbles mumblings she's never mumbled before.

Looks at the sky,
Looks to the rain.
There's that key somewhere made from good times and dancing,
The one that could lead to escape.

The real him
Lives in her wishes
Like her dad
And the daydream adventuring of boarding school,
Tuck-shops and hockey,
The soft punch of pillow fights,
Exited whispers of midnight feasts.

Has no idea she dreams,
That somewhere there's the breath of poetry.
Doesn't remember their first date, cheap booze and a crate.

Has never told him she once saved a baby from drowning.

He shouts in tongues at Mars,
Calls it the eye of the demon.
Convinced it reads his past and knows the dark of his family,
He gets scared.
Sometimes Mars shouts back,
More baleful,
More anarchic, and tells the world his secrets.
Mars is a warring oaf.
Bangs his chest and roars war at the universe.
Man in the Moon watches distant,
Unable.
Man in the Sun sizzles.

A begging and fighting combo, been on the telly,

BBC.
Broken Britain and benefit fraud.
Five minutes in a whole hour of hell.
Close-ups of their feet and her mouth mumbling babies,
Wringing hands and booze tears.
She calls it her movie debut.
He doesn't recall.
She remembers being snooty,
All Lauren Bacall and important.

Different songs at the same time,
A noise bullying calm,
Bags of broken words
Shaking like fists.
Tells her he once cut a record.
She thinks the things thrown at them are flowers,
Curtseys.

The city's enormous,
Blokey, envelops like a slate grey duvet.
Leaks amber and half-lit ghosts of alleyways,
Drums up drunken punks,
Tap dancing rats and teenage hysteria of The Beatles.

Linking arms now, tumble walking,
Dwarfed in the red scar ruptures of dawn.
Takes her to the docks,
Down to the water,
Laughing and holding on.

Taking time and white spirit,
They sit in wonder and story-telling
As the river intoxicates the land.

Folly Butler And The Blossom Of Fireworks

Some men are harbingers of Satan.

In old books of dusty grain and wheatgerm,
Amidst the intricate lettering of monks,
The Dog-Heads bark orders
From the metaphysical marrow of bones.
WOOF!
Bones pointing at and telling tales of failures of God.
They howl on the insides of the hearts of mothers,
Try to scupper their beating.
So many lies to scour truth from,
Wring sorrow.
Mothers sing to block out the din,
Scream to overcome their orders.
I've seen mothers turn banshee to stop the noise.
Do anything to keep their faith.
Seen them smash and destroy just to make sense of living.

And they bite at the ankles of women
Who've just painted their toes
And scratch at the gold
Of their rings.

In the old books of ancient lore and shadows lost
The Dog-Heads lord over the pissing of trees,
Scar the earth of buried mothers,
Dig into their legacy with a scent to attract lovers.
Scruffy old Dog-Heads lie in the shit and the blood of hope,
Wail messages, impotent of potions of eternal life,
Slaver and froth elixirs, pungent brews that fail to stave off age.

And they rip at the hair of women
Tear at their ribbons and bows
Spit in the hearths of their cakes
And curse their first born.

Folly Butler sits atop the church, wrapped around its spire,
A Rosary of fingers and prayers.
Her words a sprawl of daffodil and Scouse.
She dreams a magnificent revenge,
A blossom of fireworks
Or a promise kept,
Something pure to keep them at bay.
Incants,
"Shcrepp thipt alna. Tea and toast,
Mirriumt mirriump pilileri pilileri. Hiya luv,
Meakupt shleel. Ooer, sorry babe.
Bismmirria et Bismmirria. Chips and egg.
Bismeel bisenta. Pan of Scouse."

From reeds of lavender and wolf bane
Points a sorceress's finger.
She just might stop their mad dash of scent and snarl.

Waits with the dawn for the whisper of God
And a clean caress of spring.

The Man Crone

Some men are the black of a jackdaw's eye.

In a house,
Worn and thatched by widowed duck down,
The down of widowed ducks,
The Man Crone, cuppa dandelions and slurp slurps herbs.
Chortles and wood-chucks splinters,
Lifts the pox off cows, smooth as silks their udders
And with a shot of whisky necks their milk.
Shakes his soul-stick at clouds,
Inebriate and absorbing,
Yells like Lear at his storm daughters.

He's wet and refusing his bones,
Damns their ineffectuality,
Creak,
And memory of dancing;

Laughs at the West and its insistence on shine,
Boos the North and its petal winds,
Spits at the East and its arrogance,
Yawns at the dead of the South.
"This planet is theatre, crooked theatre."
His bellows carry an avalanche of tears and ice,
But bellows are for weathers
Choosing to fight back.

"The whimsy deep of life"
Naps with his head on the shoulder of The Devil,
Legs on the knees of God,

Tours the in-out jitterbug of dreams.
There's a woman in there,
No face and applauded in ivy.
She whispers in daffodil his name:
"Scrimpt Threpp Oomphla."

He's on first name terms with the tide.
Stretches.

Gone Fission
[for Ken Campbell, 1941-2008]

Some men are inspirational.
In 1980, Ken Campbell became artistic director of the Everyman Theatre in
Liverpool. He trailblazed and inspired in equal measure. He made Everyman
Youth Theatre people extras in The Warp, an amazing experience I can never
forget. He changed cities and lives.

In the shine of a supernova
Made blinding by Ra,
The little baby Ken shot cockney-eyed
From the cunt of a star.
He blistered and blustered formulae and theory,
He blasted and bolted and very nearly changed the world.

I think he slept in a kaleidoscope,
I think he chipped in on the wheel.

Colour!
He re-booted colour.

Clearly knew his voice,
Dearly loved to use it.
Really loved the mind,
Knew how to Blues it.

There are parades where your feet strolled,
There are ideas burning and sparking.
Teenagers who are now old
Are larking and singing your praises.

Oh, how mighty those little acorns grew.
You made us giants and children.
Giants and children, Ken,
And giants and children know.
They know!
They sit atop and stare down,
Playing.

A city sits up, hears you shriek ideas.
A city steps up to the peak of its powers.
A city opens its mouth and swallows you whole.
A city that knows base metal
Is a city that knows gold.

The Everyman became everyone
And everyone everything,
Everybody a merry dance,
Every brain cell jigging.

A total event horizon.

It was spectacular
Burning in the White Star of your love.

The jazz-bang of your theatre
Rewrites time
And I realise nuclear energy
Is human.

Human!
He re-booted human.

A Middle-Aged Muddling

Some men are middle-aged.

Turned up baggy
In scrunched scorched paper,
All brown and vinegar soaked.
Smell of gunpowder and squib.
Damp as an old idea.
A bit *Just William*,
But now.

The gym promised tum of a trampoline tenure,
Jam in the donut
Of doing.

Wait for a thought and wait for a bus,
Destination, a Vaseline fudge.
While there, in a field, a teenage you
Fucks in hollows of trees.

The "might remember this."
The "probably will do that."

Fast cars of ancient *broom, broom!*
Skid-screech a choir of discordant adventuring
And the lollypop-man is you,
Inaudibly grumbling
At the children growing older.

Promised yourself you'd be stories,
That you'd wear a cape and fly.

And When I'm Old

Some men are ageing.

And when I'm old
I'll sink to the ground and beg for redemption.
I'll let my tears be rivulets
Feeding the fire of an inflamed sea.
You'll see them as silver slipstreams
Snaking toward a regretting sun.
Believe me, they need to travel.
Don't stop them,
Be kind to them.
I think they need understanding.
If I could hold them in my hand
I'd tell them they were worthwhile
And well worth crying.
I wouldn't let them feel unworthy.
Well,
I'd do my best to.

Tears.
Soon as you try to tell them anything they disappear.

Gordon
[1964-2011]

Some men are your first love.

I can't talk to anyone and it's all very still.
The night has a way of pausing.
Wish I could talk to you.
Just to say things
And y'know I don't know what,
Just things.
That auld talk of Scottish-Scouse things,
All accents and twangs,
A lot of bluster, laughter and memory noises.

When we called each other "Pally".
When we'd hand in hand through the night.
The night was ours for a time,
A young night,
A first-love night.
I remember the stars shone brighter
And The Mersey sang shanties with a Scottish flair,
The moon and her bagpipes shrilling.

Drunken staggers and hysterics.
Your trademark,
Because you knew how to roar
And be camper, louder, bigger than a drag queen.

My mother embracing you as her own
Filled my heart.
Never thought she'd hug a gay.
Never thought she'd laugh with one.

You held her up, made her feel romance.
Never thought she'd fall in love with one.

Our Chris still loves you,
Told me last time I saw him.
Said he dreams of us back together.
Has a picture of us in Blackpool,
Looks proudly at it and smiles.

The you-prints of you,
Thumbed and fingering my memories,
A photo album of snaps I don't have.
There's one of you naked
And I'm calling you ginger-minge.

The burst of your tartan,
Colour-splashes
Daubed all over the city.
A profound and complex check
With no knickers and a whole lorra hung.
You loved the staring at your sporran.

That dark-cloud temper
Housing a stubborn
A storm couldn't shift.
A stubborn that had to be worn away
With gifts of aftershave and chocolate.
There's a different rain now
And a howling finding peace.
I think I can hear it.
The night has a way of listening.

I hope there's peace, Pally.

I hope there's calm.

I hope someone is saying
Just one of the things
I wished I could say.

The Telling Man

Some men need listening to.

Wait for him
Like you might a bus or train
And get him,
And don't stop him telling you about his secrets and joys.
One day he'll tell you about the dark corners
Where children stood, where the veil was drawn
About the door to nowhere and waiting to tell.

Let him tell you lies and believe them,
Believe them for him.
He's never more alive than when he's lying,
Never more honest and real.
Don't try to catch him out,
Don't be nasty.

He doesn't want to hurt you,
Just wants to tell stories of Hollywood and singing.
There's no real harm in that,
Just beauty between mishaps of words.
He's making monologues from wishes.
Nod in the right places
And laugh from time to time.

And let him tell you he loves you,
How much, and why.

Oh Father

Some men have faith.

Rising up, got foggy,
Depleted,
Earth boggy,
As the young footballer, soggy, petered out redemption.
Deaf ears regale his bleating.
The crack of her beatings,
His knees clutched by the clamp of carpet.
Deflated, he balloons compliment:
"Mistress is goddess."
She won't forgive him his detriment.
He is excrement on the six inch nail of her sacrament heels.
A bell without sound, he peels silently to her bitter judgement.
She's sleeping off yesterday's slaves,
Yawns away yesterday's tales
While he sets sail,
Crucifix in fist, at the Amen of his domination.

Jesus The Babe

Some men are the Son of God.

In a bubble,
Watching through soap, the floating nature of life,
Jesus The Babe takes stock
And pockets the forty winks he stole from thieves.
The thieves he'll hang with.
There's a blinking in his pockets,
Small talk and jiggling.

Jesus The Babe is giggling,
Laughing at the bumbling incompetence of cricket,
The gentle thump of linseed and willow.
He wonders slowly,
Why?

Jesus The Babe licks jangle off whispers,
Kisses chimes.
The noise around the garden
Tinkles.
It shimmers in melody and water.

Half-torn webs of spiders
Drape and backdrop talk,
Talk mirrored in reflections and mist.
It whispers long sentences,
Lends a mouth, an *I love you*.
Judas The Babe says,
"Jesus babe, I love you."

Jesus The Babe mimes in God a song wrapped melodically
Around the sorrow of mothers.

Elvis, Me And Big Bang Momma

Some men were there at the beginning.

Got this dance,
Rebel steps, and they're in debt to the blues.
Guitar feet baby,
Black throat baby.
Full,
Tilted,
Boogie.
Bad steps from hip and history,
Blood and soil,
Evilgood.

Taste feet man,
Imagination,
Journey.
Lickin' the earth and the earth drools groovy.
They rock 'n' roll a precise signature,
Drawing on love,
Splash!
And leave in a mirror an imprint of
Elvis and me.

And Elvis says,
"Gerry, sometimes you gotta move.
Makes you forget things bin bad,
Things bin sad and you, the wind and me,
We're brothers."

Elvis and me gotta bike,

Purrs the kitten of Joplin and rides skies never seen,
Skies never drawn.
Elvis says,
"They ain't invented this colour yet,
Still think red is angry,
Still think pink is calm.
It's a rock 'n' roll pallet baby,
You gotta know The Blues before you can paint.
Blue is gold honey.
Blue is bread.
Blue is that second before a smile."

Elvis and me talk to my grandmother,
Listen in awe.
She makes the war sound beautiful.

Elvis's lip is a roller-coaster and I'm sat in a carriage,
Arms in the air.
The dip's his throat,
He's screamin' Ghost Train.
I'm in The Sound.
Yell of God.
I'm hurtling into nowhere,
The First Dance.

And Elvis sings
"Big Bang Momma,
Birth of the Blues,

Any old way you choose."

Slap

Some men don't pull punches.

Slap.
A hard-handed wallop of how it was,
Can never be,
How it is.
It's the back of fists punctuating,
Silver sliding through the slime of your need.
Thirty fucking squiggly pieces,
No less.

Pain shines my face.
Bitter glitters,
Grimaces excuses,
It's gurning Hollywood teeth.

THWACK!

I'm running out of revolving doors,
Out of revolution,
And into cold stone wood.

Smile sweet-cheeks, smile.

You're winning.

I keep getting slapped by you.

The Magician

Some men are bleak.
This is about showbiz men. You know the type, they dominate Saturday night
TV with their smug insufferable bile. I imagine this poem is from the camp
point of view of a researcher who is moved to despair by the decline of
television. They exist.

Shadow sharp as a razor blade grin,
Pin-point splitting and rhinestoned.
Every glimmer a shine-post to perfection,
Every glamour a wish.
There's method in his madness as he spells out his walk,
Incants his talk.
It's an olde language
Full of molten words meaning apocalypse.

He knows we're scared to look and listen
In case we disappear.
Knows we're not truly confident in being queer.
Too hotchpotch, higgledy-piggledy,
Old schooled, politically too ensconced in our own malady
To realistically take him on.
And if he could magic it right
He wouldn't.
We're not young enough,
Buff enough,
Tough nor potentially rich enough to wave his wand.

The Magician chooses the assistants
He'll regale on shards of cocaine.
Assistants he'll impale on stories of speed and infamy.
Too busy cleaning up his act

To notice the mess he's made.

In dreams, The Magician owns everything,
Rules his kingdom with a rod of style.
Ingredients labelled exquisitely,
Champagne ladled languidly into mouths miming longingly
His songs.

Dreams real,
Beat hypnotic.
There's intent in his gesticulations.
Knows how to enchant,
Knows disco is voodoo,
The floor punching power of bass.
Entertains the potency of powders and potions
Eating the dance floor,
Living the dream.

Bruise of night and lure of moon, a dollar shiny
In the ink of cash.
So protected even truth can't scratch.
Yes,
He eats babies and yes,
He steals souls, but they're offered.
He never asks.
The Magician never asks.
Chooses.
Basks.

And perhaps there are no charms to protect your children,
Rhymes or prayers.

The Magician has no sadness or fear of regret.

Hovers like an angel above responsibility.
A tooth in Satan's smile,
Demon drool made manifest.
Victorian and post modern,
Jack the Ripper and modems.
The butt of a joke he loves to laugh at uncontrollably.

Because he'll sit on your TV and murder your children
And you will let him murder your children.
You will applaud him murdering your children.
You will laugh as he murders your children,
Hypnotised totally.

"Hubble bubble
Toil and trouble."

The Magician
Sinks into the belly of his magic
As Disney animation
Tickles him to sleep.

Cake

Some men have no intention to stop.

How did The Man get so greedy?
Did he see the world like a great big cake
Baked just for him and the people he owns?
Crumbs!
Did he think all that cream could cleanse his soul?
A pussy milk, soured thick and curdling,
Bubbling intensely like the festering larder of a cannibalistic
B-movie monster.
A monster made from dead men, sultanas and bit part actors,
Baked to disorder and imperfection
By a misguided mad professor.
A misguided mad professor
Determined to imitate the greatness and perfection of God.

Did he think he could hide that sweet sticky stink
With a pomander,
Hysterically squealed from a make-over show?
A pomander reimagined from leftover Christmas cake,
Armageddon and crackers.
You know the make-over show I mean,
The one with the two camp pretenders trilling overdose
And oblivion in television Scots.
How did The Man decide on this?
Och-Aye the noo!

When did he think it was a good idea to see people
Who might be great artists or builders
Grovel for cake or beg for what's left
Of the very last bits of the rotting cow?

When did he think this was a good thing to teach his children?
When did The Man decide other men
Could not be great artists or builders?

Is there a time somewhere I don't know
Where The Man stood alone
Atop his ivory tower and declared to the world
That his voice
Would be the only voice obeyed?
In that same time-space I don't know,
Did all the other men agree?
Was The Man's name God
Or Tony
Or Rupert
Or Margaret
Or Adolph,
Chuck or Rod,
Or a name made unpronounceable
By the very evil of its nature?
A name with more letters than there are scars in the sky,
Filth in the sea.
A name that created wanting in our hearts.
A name that carved hollow into empty.
There are names so old they can no longer be spoken,
Ask the lipless and invisible.
Oh dear!

When did The Man kneel
To the prissy blonde homicide of cash?
Why did he kiss it full on the mouth and call it "Sugar?"
Why did he get so greedy wanting more cake
And decorate it the way he did?
Why did The Man rape and murder or murder and rape
[take your pick]

Those children in the concentration camp
And why did other men cheer
And why does it still go on?

How much cake can any man want?

"Someone left the cake out in the rain
I don't think that I can take it
'Cos it took so long to bake it."

Crumbs!

Of Men

Some men are men.

In a haberdashery of muscle and sinew
And conveyor junk of cuddly toys,
Men firm up to what they never were,
What they never could be.
Deep thought buried in emotion,
Buried by demons, buried by deed.

Perhaps men's empathy can not be words.
Perhaps men's empathy is just that.
Perhaps men's empathy can not be questioned.

All men are therapists.
All women are therapists.

Of men there are stories,
Carrying worlds and parting waves.
Of men there are fathers,
Scuffed knees and runny nosed.
Of men there are mountain tops,
Abominable,
Unsure.
Of men there are oceans,
Shoals,
Black.

I'm sometimes by the river, by willow, and men are swans.
A midsummer shiver of down and white,
A question mark neck of where is our elegance.

By the river I realize how protected and loved I've been
By fist and wing.
By the river men frisk and giggle with sons and daughters.
By the river they are,
And they are not,
Men.

In anvil strike and glass-blowing spark of heat,
Sweat and industry of men,
I marvel at the structures they created,
Fell from,
Died for and celebrated,
Their red brick comment and dust-cloud weight.

The killing field bloodbath shit pants stench,
Mud blood mouths and can't believe of why is war.
I grieve for the grief they weren't allowed.
I wish I could scale the bottomless pit
Of the bottomless pits,
Of the history
Of histories
Of men.

Of downward spirals and devil traps
And insides of insides gnawing at insides of insides,
Clawing at fathers and mothers,
Needing mothers and fathers,
Punching,
Suckling whores and dirt-man.
Goal!
Men of jealousy, of weakness,
Fear.
Soiled and bruised blue boy of not being solid,

Of being sold down the Swanny,
Crumbling and guffawing.
Men made of knitting,
Men made of football.
Cumming too quickly, not coming at all.
Men of baby steps and delight,
Giant steps and babies,
Sanities and crazies.
Of always nevers and maybes.
Cradling,
Adventure yarned,
Saving,
Grabbing, letting go,
Failing,
Falling.
Scalded and scolding.
Holding on to failing,
Failing to hold.
Unloved, loved too much,
Too camp, too butch,
Arms not strong enough,
Legs too weak.
Of earth not grounded,
Falling and digging to the centre of the Earth,
Pounded to a core of molten man,
Knowing far too much about not knowing.
Lava hot and glowing.

I have an image of a man stood burning inside the sun.
He is crying and if he doesn't stop soon
The sun will go out.

Bangs His Chest And Roars War At The Universe

a play in one act
by Gerry Potter

Characters:

Jesus Christ......................*Catholic saviour of souls*

Fanny Du' Nile, Queen of the Vile......*Hideous East End drag queen*

Griff the Gruff...............*Hard-nosed Scouse scally*

Folly Butler..*Herself*

Scene: *Anyone familiar with my play* Miracle *may recognize this as something of a celestial prequel. Jesus Christ and Fanny Du' Nile, the notorious ultra-cockney East-End Queen of the Vile, are sat in a beautiful garden. It is extraordinarily scented and calm. They're discussing Fanny's favourite topic, the size of men's penises.*

Fanny: So, in a nutshell Jesus, the bigger the better for me.

Jesus: I've just not really thought about it. It is of absolutely no consequence to me. I honestly have no issue with the size of anybody's penis. The girth or, indeed Fanny, how swollen the glans may get when exited.

Fanny: I'm guessing that's 'cos you're hung.

Jesus: Fanny!

Fanny: People what are hung always say that 'cos they got nothin' to be frightened of. Now, if you weren't hung you'd be all defensive and squeaky like a little girl claiming dominance over a dolls house with her ringlets all a-fire. You'd be all petulant and pouting, a Minnie Mouse speed-freak what's lost her cheese.

Jesus: I've certainly nothing to be ashamed of, but it's not that big, Fanny.

Fanny: What?

Jesus: I'm not that, what is it you say, hung?

Fanny: Oh you will be dear, mark my words, you'll be hung all right, every cunt round 'ere knows that. *[Fanny laughs raucously]*

Jesus: Oh Fanny, you and your tawdry vaudeville. Punchy it most certainly is, charming it's not. Original it will never be.

Fanny: Just pullin' yer leg big guy. 'Ere, 'ave you seen my acrylics? I've just had 'em re-gemmed. *[Fanny shows Jesus her newly decorated false fingernails]*

Jesus: They're wonderful Fanny, a real display of Aztec wit and savagery. They're fine, really fine.

Fanny: 'Ere Jesus, be a love, do us a favour would ye darlin', show us yours?

Jesus: I don't have any new nails, Fanny.

Fanny: Oh you will do dear, mark my words, you'll 'ave nails alright, every cunt round 'ere knows that. No-one's gonna 'ave more nails than you. *[Fanny laughs raucously again]*

Jesus: Fanny, your childish preoccupation with my impending doom is wearing linen thin, so it is. How many times do I have to tell you? This is Heaven, not the Vauxhall Tavern.

Fanny: You're not angry with me, are ye darlin'?

Jesus: No, I'm not.

Fanny: You're not what?

Jesus: I'm not cross.

Fanny: Oh you will be dear, mark my words, no cunt's gonna be more cross than you, that's for sure. You're gonna be crosser than a hot-cross bun, ask any cunt. Any cunt who knows how cross a hot-cross bun is knows for sure how cross you're gonna be. Don't bear thinkin' about, so it doesn't. Crosser than a hot cross-dresser sittin' on a hot-cross bun, that's absolutely for fuckin' sure. *[Fanny laughs raucously. Her laughter sounds like a hoarse pterodactyl with emphysema, lost and directionless in an echo chamber]*

Jesus: If you weren't so charming Fanny, you'd be impossible.

Fanny: 'Ere!

Jesus: You're a delightful conundrum, Ms Du' Nile. Sometimes not having a clue what you're saying allows me to see right through you, a stained glass window that you most certainly are.

Fanny: Cheek!

Jesus: Very stained.

Fanny: Don't get all pious on me sheep-shagger, just 'cos I've out-bitched you again.

Jesus: How many times must I tell you, Fanny? A nature as forgiving as mine can't be scratched by any amount of paranoid bitching. You forget sometimes, I've taken on the might of Satan and I assure you he's not backwards in coming forwards when it comes to a sparky put down.

Fanny: But you'll always win him dear.

Jesus: Why's that Fanny?

Fanny: You know full well.

Jesus: No, I don't.

Fanny: You fuckin' do. You just want me to say it.

Jesus: Say what?

Fanny: You cunt, you know full well what. Everyone's talkin' about it.

Jesus: Fanny, I…

Fanny: What you like, you irksome little bleeder?

Jesus: Honestly, I have no idea.

Fanny: Yes, you do.

Jesus: Cross my heart and hope to resurrect.

Fanny: Give me a break Jesus love.

Jesus: Sometimes Fanny, you exasperate me.

Fanny: 'Cos you've got the bigger dick, ain'tcha!

Jesus: Oh Fanny, really.

Fanny: You absolute compliment milkin' bleeder. What you like. Honestly!

Jesus: Well, rumours are he's not packing it.

Fanny: He ain't, that's for sure.

Jesus: What makes you say that?

Fanny: I started the rumours.

Jesus: How do you know?

Fanny: Guess!

Jesus: Fanny, no!

Fanny: Fanny, yes.

Jesus: Fanny, your labyrinthine desire for darkness and pain could warrant its own Bible.

Fanny: Knew it wouldn't be long before you started judgin'.

[Pause]

Jesus: Well?

Fanny: Well what?

Jesus: You know…

Fanny: What?

Jesus: Oh come on Fanny!

Fanny: You wanna know just how big it is, don'tcha?

Jesus: Well, *dur*! If I was to say I wasn't curious I'd be lying and we both know I can't do that. So, go on… How big?

Fanny: Thought you were meant to be above all that.

Jesus: Just because I've no substantial interest in mine doesn't mean I can't relish the diminutive nature of his. He's put me through quite a tangle of tangible depressions, that one.

Fanny: Well, I didn't need lube that's for sure.

Jesus: Really! Tell me more.

Fanny: I had to ask three times if he was in.

Jesus: *Yesssss!*

Fanny: Hark at you spring lambing all over your own paradise.

Jesus: How big exactly?

Fanny: Two and a half inches.

Jesus: *Noooooo!!!*

Fanny: And that's hard as well. I swear. May you strike me down dead if I'm lying. Me acrylics were longer.

Jesus: Two and a half fucking inches hard. Brilliant! You know the way he swaggers around, you've seen him strutting like he's got a whole black pudding down there. Tosser! Absolute fucking tosser! Two and a half inches, get in there sister, goal! Satan's got a weener, Satan's got a weener. Oh Fanny, you've made an immortal deity very happy. It's like all my Christmases have come at once.

Fanny: Should do dear, you invented the fuckin' thing.

Jesus: Would you Adam and Eve it, Satan's got a weener. How mint is that? Whoooo hooooo!

[Fanny suddenly stops]

Fanny: 'Ere Jesus, stop muckin' about.

Jesus: What's up Fanny?

Fanny: Can't you hear it?

Jesus: What?

Fanny: That crunchin' noise.

Jesus: Yes, yes I can. What is it?

Fanny: It's 'orrible.

Jesus: Sounds like the unholy roar of engines.

Fanny: The all pervadin' sound of doom, if you ask me.

Jesus: Definitely engines. Or some sort of machinery.

Fanny: Machines here? They're not allowed are they?

Jesus: At any cost. Paradise for God's sake.

Fanny: Come on, let's find out.

[They hurriedly set off. Jesus suddenly stops]

Jesus: You're not lying to me Fanny, two and a half inches?

Fanny: Oh come on!

A little ahead from Fanny and Jesus in a clearing, Griff the Gruff is toiling away at his construction. He is putting the finishing touches to a multi-storey tower block called John F. Kennedy Heights.

Griff: There, that should do it. Tell ye what Griff, you've done a brilliant job mate, even if you do say so yourself. If this doesn't get you out, nothin' will.

Fanny: *[Entering]* I shoulda known, Griff the fuckin' Gruff. Up to yer old tricks again, ye mangy Scouse cunt?

Griff: Christ, look what the cat dragged in. A shagged out Cleopatra. Oh, and would you believe it, Christ.

Jesus: Griff, what in Heaven's name are you doing?

Griff: Sumthin' I should've done some time ago.

Fanny: What, killed yourself?

Griff: Already dead luv. And so, sadly, are you.

Jesus: What is it?

Fanny: It's a tower block, ye numpty.

Jesus: It's monstrous, utterly monstrous.

Griff: It's nearly thirteen floors mate, just one more to go.

Fanny: Unlucky for some.

Griff: Unlucky for you in a minute, ye snide little bitch.

Fanny: 'Ere!

Jesus: But Griff, you're in Paradise. What on earth are you doing this for?

Griff: Got bored with clouds an' 'arps.

Jesus: You're not an angel, Griff. Only angels have clouds an' 'arps— *harps*!

Griff: Got bored with Heaven.

Jesus: This is meant to be a transcendental idyll, Griff. A safe time-space for the soul, a transformative reconfiguration of body to spirit. This is the vessel of super-nature, not a council estate.

Griff: Just wanted a few home comforts, a poky pot-smokin' lager stinkin' living room, thumpin' with Led Zep and Jeremy Kyle.

Jesus: You're trying to turn Heaven into Liverpool.

Griff: Needs a bit of a face lift if ask me, too leafy, stinks of grapes and brie. It's like Putney.

Fanny: No cunt's asking you what you think, are they?

Griff: Shut ye mouth gorgon, before I shut it for ye.

Jesus: Griff, I can't allow this.

Griff: So!

Jesus: What do you mean by "So"?

Griff: So warra ye gonna do about it?

Jesus: First, I'm going to ask you to take it down.

Griff: Fuck off!

Jesus: Take it down.

Griff: Do one, knob'ead.

Jesus: If you don't...

Griff: What...

Jesus: I shall have to cast you down.

Griff: Don't give a toss. I'd rather burn eternally than yawn forever.

Jesus: Hell isn't a fire hazard, Griff. It's the never ending screech of a soul in turmoil. The most agonizing pain imaginable, something you shouldn't take lightly.

Griff: There's nothin' for me to do here, man of God, it's borin', an' nothin's more agonizin' than bein' bored. I don't belong here, there's nothing to lie about, no cars to steal, no bus shelters to smash. There's no fuckin' busses mate.

Jesus: Take it down.

Fanny: You heard.

Griff: No!

Jesus: I think you're forgetting who you're talking to.

Griff: I think your forgetting I don't give a fuck.

Jesus: The eternal agony of the underrated and talentless will be as nothing compared to what awaits you down there.

Griff: For such a gangster Jesus, you're a very unconvincin' gangster. I stopped being frightened of you when I was seven.

Jesus: Take it down now. I command it.

Griff: It's my tower block and it's stayin' up. I built this with my own hands; I didn't magic it with a wave of my imagination. Blood, sweat and tears mate. Blood, sweat an' fuckin' tears.

Jesus: You leave me no choice.

Griff: I'm ready for whatever you throw at me.

Fanny: I can't wait to see the back of ye, that's for sure.

Griff: Can't say I'm gonna miss you either, ye skank. Go on Jesus, do your worst.

[Jesus raises his arms dramatically. He looks dark biblical and threatening; he is about to bellow when he suddenly distracted]

Jesus: What's that?

Griff: What's what, what you pointin' at?

Jesus: That in your tracksuit.

Griff: It's me idiot, I'm in me tracksuit.

Fanny: Oh my God! Fuckin' Nora, I ain't noticed that before.

Griff: What?

Jesus: Is that your penis, Griff?

Griff: Yeah, what of it?

Fanny: It's fuckin' enormous, that's what. What a trouser snake.

Jesus: I say Griff, rather a lot of ballast on that raft, that's for sure.

Griff: Jesus, you pervin' my dick?

Jesus: No, not perving, just taken aback that's all. I've never seen one quite so, well, obvious. Is it real?

Griff: Course it is.

Jesus: Cripes!

Fanny: I'll say. If I'd known you were packin' a submarine darlin', I'd've well dived down by now. Drag-queen overboard! Drag-queen overboard! Oooh, help me, help me, I think I've lost my asp.

Griff: Shit! It's these trackies. I don't normally wear them, show everything off.

Fanny: Well, you've got nothin' to be ashamed of dear, that's for sure. Never mind bananas, it's like you've got a whole barrer load of apples and pears down there. *[Laughs hysterically, almost to an invisible audience. She almost hears them laughing back]*

Griff: What's goin' on here? I'm buildin' a thirteen storey block of flats in the middle of Paradise in order to be relegated to Hell and you two can't stop gawpin' at me cock. It's just a fuckin' dick.

Jesus: Oh it's more than that, Griff. It's the dick of dicks.

Fanny: Say that again. Last time I saw something that big was in my dreams and even then it wasn't as big as that. You got African blood in ye?

Jesus: Fanny, don't be so rude. Your stereotyping preoccupations are, as per usual, wildly inaccurate. I didn't just bestow big penises on Afro-Caribbeans, the Danish and the Irish. I tried to share them out evenly. But this one just must've slipped through. I would never have burdened a mere mortal with such a preternatural appendage.

Fanny: Why?

Jesus: Well, because…

Fanny: Go on.

Jesus: Well...

Fanny: Well!

Jesus: It's none of your business.

Fanny: Oh, I get it!

Jesus: What?

Fanny: With great dicks comes great responsibility.

Jesus: What are you wittering?

Fanny: The cock is everything, all hail the cock!

Jesus: Crystal-Meth and rent-boys have driven you insane.

Fanny: Lookin' a bit green-eyed there, Jesus.

Jesus: Will someone save me from the damaged ramblings of this Egyptian scrubber.

Fanny: It's bigger than yours, innit?

Jesus: Fanny, really!

Fanny: It is, innit?

Jesus: Shhh!

Fanny: I get it now. You bein' the human manifestation of God, thought you'd got the biggest dick in the history of history, didn't ya?

Jesus: It's complicated.

Fanny: Oh I see, this one must've just slipped through when you were 'avin' an off day. You an' your other two selves musta dozed off or summink.

Jesus: Assumptions are a loser's way of answering questions.

Fanny: All this crap about you not bein' interested in the size of anybody's penis was just you gloating to yourself, 'cos all the time you thought you had the biggest penis. No wonder you were dancin' your sandals off when I told you about Satan. You fuckin' hypocrite.

Griff: What's goin' on?

Fanny: Him, that's what's goin' on.

Jesus: And I've every right to go on.

Fanny: 'Ere we go.

Jesus: You've no idea Fanny, the weight of ultimate responsibility, the cavernous aloneness of perfection, the nagging perpetuity of grace. I can't fall in love or play football, can't even get my hand under Mary Magdalene's bra - and she's a prozzy. It's just this, being just this. Just being, supremely being. Always right, always listening, always forgiving. Everything about me has to be the best it can possibly be. You can't let them down. You don't hear the millions of desperate pleas every second. "Take away this cancer", "Save my child", "A bubble-butt, please Lord, a bubble-butt", the turgid plodding of the human race, it's enough to drive you to the bleakest insanity. If you could imagine the feeling of eternal erosion, but never actually eroding, then you would get into knowing only a trillionth of what it's like to be me. On top of that, I have to appear humble. I have look like I don't want anything, that I share everything. And I don't want anything, Fanny, and I do share everything, but there has to be something that's mine. Something I can call mine.

Fanny: Your dick?

Jesus: Yes, my dick!

Griff: Are you for real?

Jesus: 'Fraid so.

Griff: A big dick?

Jesus: Yes, a big fucking dick. There, it's out. I wanted the biggest dick in the universe, dirty, nasty old Jesus. I know, why don't you crucify me or something? Oh, don't worry, you will. I wanted something for me Fanny, for me. The only thing in the whole of creation I ever wanted. These robes would always hide any tell-tale bulge, no-one need ever know. I'd just be humble all powerful Jesus, the easiest person to talk to, no matter how shy you are. The benign conduit between Earth and Heaven, your best friend and saviour. "Here everybody, have all the loaves, here's all the fish. Dead are we? Never mind, up you rise and off you pop." Forever giving, never being vain or selfish and always looking like Robert Powell. But I'm a bloody man, Fanny, I'm still a man. The only flesh and blood part of this god-forsaken triumvirate and like all men I've got needs.

Fanny: Just goes to show ya, no cunt's perfect are they.

Griff: Jesus, I didn't know it was that big a deal.

Jesus: Yes, it is Griff. It is that big a deal.

Griff: It's only a dick.

Jesus: No, Griff. It's the biggest dick, and now it's yours not mine.

Fanny: I'll never forget what my old mate Ava Banana used to say. She was a wise old cow.

Jesus: What?

Fanny: Ava was this drag queen from Essex and her gimmick was two giant bananas stuck to the top of her head, hence the name. She had these two inflatable bananas and what might have been melons for ear-rings, could've been pineapples or mangoes, who cares. Anyway, she'd just do her act which was straight forward drag, some mime, then a bit of patter, maybe a bit of audience participation if she weren't too pissed. One day, I asked her, I said, "Ava, what's with the giant bananas on the top of your head?" And she said, "If I'm gonna spend the rest of my life entertaining a group of cock obsessed eternal teenagers then I want them subliminally to know it. Gays, Fanny," she said, "just a bunch of colourful dicks." And then she took a last swig of her double Bacardi and died right there in front of me. That was the last thing she said, a philosopher and bitch in equal measure. I'm pretty sure she's downstairs.

Jesus: What's that got to with anything?

Fanny: It's all your fuckin' fault, ain't it?

Jesus: What is?

Fanny: The state of the human race. You're meant to be perfect ain'tcha, but ye not. You wantin' the biggest dick in the universe somehow seeped through to them. Now they all want the biggest dicks. What's in the bitch, Jesus, come out in the pups. They've all got the residual arrogance of your vanity. You're the ultimate colourful dick.

Jesus: I'm not gay, Fanny.

Fanny: You don't have to be gay to be a colourful dick sweetheart, it just helps.

Griff: You mean the inherent weakness in all men is because he couldn't come clean about 'avin' a big dick?

Fanny: Not just a big dick, Griff, oh no, the biggest dick.

Griff: Fuckin' 'ell!

Fanny: Now there's an original sin, you might say.

Jesus: It's more complicated than that, Griff. I wasn't supposed to have any vanity.

Fanny: But ya did, didn't ya?

Jesus: Yes, I did, and now even that's taken a battering. Mine's the second biggest dick in the universe. Who'd've thought I'd be usurped by a Scouser.

Griff: I'm not arsed about 'avin' a bigger dick than you, Jesus. I just built this tower block to piss you off so you would relegate me to Hell. So wave ye magic wand or whatever and send me on me way.

Jesus: No!

Griff: What?

Jesus: Absolutely not. You're staying put, Mr Gruff.

Griff: Why?

Jesus: I can't send you down there. I'd be a laughing stock. Satan can't have the biggest penis in the universe on his side.

Griff: I'm sure Satan's got a pretty big dick of his own, hasn't he? After all, he is Satan.

Jesus: No, Griff, he's cursed with the penis of a cherub.

Griff: Christ!

Jesus: Now you see my dilemma, if I put you down there...

Griff: The power shifts.

Jesus: Exactly.

Griff: See what ye mean kidder.

Fanny: Jesus, what's that, you sweatin' blood?

Jesus: Always do at times like this.

Fanny: Vile!

[Jesus screams]

Jesus: You are such a torment, Fanny!

[Silence]

Griff: Well, I'm not gonna take me tower block down. We like what we like, don't we. We need what we need and I need somewhere to chill.

Jesus: *[Pulling himself together]* That's ok.

Griff: Sorry?

Jesus: You don't have to take it down.

Griff: Thought it was against all the laws of Paradise.

Jesus: No-one will notice one tower block, I'm sure.

Fanny: It's pretty big, Jesus love.

Jesus: If having the tower block means you'll stay here in Heaven, then so be it.

Fanny: Beginning of the end sweetheart. He's got his tower block, some other cunt will want a bettin' shop. Won't be long before there's a gay sauna, mark my words. Chippies, casinos, pound shops…

Jesus: I need him on my side, Fanny. You wouldn't understand, it's a bloke thing.

Fanny: I am a fuckin' bloke.

Jesus: Yeah, whatever.

Griff: Sorry, Jesus la.

Jesus: Yeah, whatever.

Griff: No, honestly, I mean it. I've got no deal with the size of anybody's dick, honest.

Fanny: Save it Griff, I had that conversation wiv him before.

Griff: What conversation?

Fanny: The "you're all a bunch of liars" conversation.

Griff: Fuck off, Fanny. Jesus, you alright?

Jesus: It's ok, I'll be fine. If you both don't mind I need a bit of alone time.

Fanny: First time I've seen him like this. Look what you've gone an' done now, Griff the Gruff. They're the tears that he's meant to be shedding at Gethsemane.

Griff: Look mate, if you fancy a pint of ambrosia later on, give us a shout.

Jesus: Maybe. See how I feel.

Fanny: Yeah, come round in a bit love. I'll do "Nathan Jones" by Bananarama for ya, that'll cheer you up.

Jesus: Thank you, Fanny.

Fanny: Well, Jesus, Griff an' me, we're gonna tear down our North-South divide, as it were. Aren't we, my enormous python?

Griff: Are we? I still can't stand ye.

Fanny: Clasp yer hands round me little asp would ye, there's a love.

Griff: Couldn't think of anything more 'orrible.

Fanny: Griff, sweetheart, you've got summink I want and I've just had me acrylics re-gemmed. Believe me darlin', you're in for a good time.

[They leave. Jesus is sitting alone. He is eventually joined by Folly Butler. She is both physical and ethereal. She shimmers between light and solidity. Her face changes constantly from an elfin beauty to an old crone. She sits gently with him]

Folly: Mirrililli phrep etisoo.

Jesus: Oh, Folly.

Folly: Tiriepp shter shom.

Jesus: It's been a day.

Folly: Shtelp.

Jesus: Thank you.

Folly: Leshta pheld.

Jesus: Yes, something like that.

Folly: Pishmool.

Jesus: It's serious.

Folly: Pishmool.

Jesus: Saying it twice won't make it any better.

Folly: Shlaft.

Jesus: Sorry for snapping, Folly.

Folly: Bickelikker.

Jesus: I've messed up, or rather, been caught out.

Folly: Milleeta et birmieeia atle tuli pilute metren aldo bersemirria akt schleel.

Jesus: Ah Folly, your daffodil musing enchants as ever, always wise and musical. There are times though, my little fairy, even they fail to enliven my heart.

Folly: shclerta shelpith.

Jesus: I died today, Folly. Not the agony of a crowd baying crucifixion. I died the death of honesty, the unforgiving death of self.

Folly: Chlacht.

Jesus: Chlacht indeed, but so much more than that, the eternal balance of everything spinning into chaos for starters. Not the good chaos of the beginnings of galaxies, much smaller and much bigger than that. The niggling chaos of doubt and confusion, the howling chaos of paranoia and vanity. I've whispered secrets without ears and with all the ears. Cataclysmic chatterings splattering around a black hole of mine's bigger than yours and yours doesn't matter. Greed where there's no money, selfishness without mirrors. It's a ball rolling all right and I've pushed it. Gathering all the "it's not importants" as it thunders. I should've known and, to be honest, I did know and what did I do? I did *it*, that's what I did, *it*, the infernal eternal *it*. I backtracked my own poetry so I could give off a good reflection. Chlacht! I wish I could. I'm not you, Folly.

Folly: Terbirismelpt ogla shthool.

Jesus: Easy to chirrup from where you're sitting. I've failed, Folly, and I've got to carry on living in the thick of it. Drown in the thick of it and ultimately learn how to enjoy the thick of it. Those poor bastards down there, all not good enough while they wipe out cities. Too good to simply love and it's all down to me, not happy with my lot when I had it all. I just wanted it bigger than anybody else's, Folly.

Folly: Mesheltha spids sponel.

Jesus: What have I done?

Folly: Beteshmek ekekek.

Jesus: Maybe there's something I can do.

Folly: Peshtalia shmelts ifiniastum.

Jesus: I know I've already done too much, but I am Jesus, Folly.

Folly: Mesma!

Jesus: Maybe I can bestow on the world one last great miracle, a miracle that ends prejudice. Create a wider understanding.

Folly: Geshtalia mirriumpa plesa.

Jesus: Use what I've learnt today to make it all right. Use the lessons Folly, use the lessons.

Folly: Mirrlia mirrellia shpelet.

Jesus: A mixture of Fanny's wisdom and Griff's heavenly down to earthness. A miracle of such magnitude it sorts everything out.

Folly: Scertipul chlecht evissimia.

Jesus: You're right Folly, you're right. I'm a silly marauder.

Folly: Teshatia sleel.

Jesus: I feel such a fool.

Folly: Fleepa.

[There is a long still silence]

Jesus: What are we Folly, what are we?

  The End